T0383164

Technical Innovation, Solving the Data Spaces and Marketplaces Interoperability Problems for the Global Data-Driven Economy

i3-MARKET Series - Part III: The i3-MARKET FOSS Handbook

RIVER PUBLISHERS SERIES IN COMPUTING AND INFORMATION SCIENCE AND TECHNOLOGY

Series Editors:

K.C. CHEN
National Taiwan University, Taipei, Taiwan
University of South Florida, USA

SANDEEP SHUKLA
Virginia Tech, USA
Indian Institute of Technology Kanpur, India

The "River Publishers Series in Computing and Information Science and Technology" covers research which ushers the 21st Century into an Internet and multimedia era. Networking suggests transportation of such multimedia contents among nodes in communication and/or computer networks, to facilitate the ultimate Internet.

Theory, technologies, protocols and standards, applications/services, practice and implementation of wired/wireless networking are all within the scope of this series. Based on network and communication science, we further extend the scope for 21st Century life through the knowledge in machine learning, embedded systems, cognitive science, pattern recognition, quantum/biological/molecular computation and information processing, user behaviors and interface, and applications across healthcare and society.

Books published in the series include research monographs, edited volumes, handbooks and textbooks. The books provide professionals, researchers, educators, and advanced students in the field with an invaluable insight into the latest research and developments.

Topics included in the series are as follows:-

- Artificial intelligence
- Cognitive Science and Brian Science
- Communication/Computer Networking Technologies and Applications
- Computation and Information Processing
- Computer Architectures
- Computer networks
- Computer Science
- Embedded Systems
- Evolutionary computation
- Information Modelling
- Information Theory
- Machine Intelligence
- Neural computing and machine learning
- Parallel and Distributed Systems
- Programming Languages
- Reconfigurable Computing
- Research Informatics
- Soft computing techniques
- Software Development
- Software Engineering
- Software Maintenance

For a list of other books in this series, visit www.riverpublishers.com

i3-MARKET

Technical Innovation, Solving the Data Spaces and Marketplaces Interoperability Problems for the Global Data-Driven Economy

i3-MARKET Series - Part III: The i3-MARKET FOSS Handbook

Editors

Martín Serrano

Achille Zappa

Waheed Ashraf

Pedro Maló

Márcio Mateus

Edgar Fries

Iván Martínez

Alessandro Amicone

Justina Bieliauskaite

Marina Cugurra

Routledge
Taylor & Francis Group

LONDON AND NEW YORK

Published 2024 by River Publishers

River Publishers

Alsbjergvej 10, 9260 Gistrup, Denmark

www.riverpublishers.com

Distributed exclusively by Routledge

4 Park Square, Milton Park, Abingdon, Oxon OX14 4RN

605 Third Avenue, New York, NY 10017, USA

Technical Innovation, Solving the Data Spaces and Marketplaces Interoperability Problems for the Global Data-Driven Economy / by Martín Serrano, Achille Zappa, Waheed Ashraf, Pedro Maló, Márcio Mateus, Edgar Fries, Iván Martínez, Alessandro Amicone, Justina Bieliauskaite, Marina Cugurra.

ISBN: 978-87-7004-173-7 (hardback)

978-10-4009-244-6 (online)

978-10-0349-884-1 (master ebook)

DOI: 10.1201/9788770041737

i3-MARKET

Contents

Preface   xi

Who Should Read this Book?   xiii

What is Addressed in the i3-MARKET Book Series?   xv

What is Covered in this i3-MARKET Part III Book?   xvii

Acknowledgements   xix

List of Figures   xxi

List of Tables   xxv

List of Contributors   xxvii

List of Abbreviations   xxxi

1   i3-MARKET Overview   1
    1.1   Context   1

2   General Description   3
    2.1   Deployment and Operational Concepts   3
          2.1.1   Consider the requirements of the software   3
          2.1.2   Evaluate the deployment environment   3
          2.1.3   Consider automation and orchestration   4
          2.1.4   Evaluate containerization options   4

		2.1.5	Consider monitoring and reporting tools	4
	2.2		Deployment Specification	4
	2.3		Terminology	5
	2.4		i3-MARKET Artifacts Overview	6
	2.5		Deployment Architecture View	8
	2.6		i3-MARKET Network Infrastructure	10
	2.7		Software Stack	10
	2.8		i3-MARKET Master Environment	12
	2.9		i3-MARKET Pilot Environment	15

3 Backplane API Gateway — **19**

3.1 Objectives ... 19
3.2 Solution Design/Blocks ... 20
   3.2.1 Authentication and authorization ... 20
      3.2.1.1 Authentication ... 21
      3.2.1.2 Authorization ... 22
   3.2.2 Subsystem implementation ... 23
   3.2.3 Data flows ... 24
   3.2.4 Service Integration Manager ... 24
   3.2.5 Automatic integration mechanism ... 25
   3.2.6 Subsystem OAS repository ... 25
   3.2.7 Backplane repository ... 26
      3.2.7.1 Remote images ... 27
   3.2.8 Final deployment ... 28
   3.2.9 Multiple environments support ... 29
3.3 Interfaces ... 31
   3.3.1 Developers ... 31
   3.3.2 OIDC discovery ... 31
   3.3.3 OIDC core ... 31
   3.3.4 RegistryBlockchainController ... 31
   3.3.5 RegistryController ... 32
   3.3.6 AuthController ... 32
   3.3.7 Conflict-resolver service ... 32
   3.3.8 FarewellController ... 32
   3.3.9 HelloController ... 33
   3.3.10 OpenApiController ... 33
   3.3.11 Notifications ... 33
   3.3.12 Queues ... 34
   3.3.13 Subscriptions ... 34

3.3.14 PingController 35
3.3.15 Cost-controller 35
3.3.16 Price-controller 35
3.3.17 RatingService 36
3.3.18 Agreement 36
3.3.19 Explicit user consent 37
3.3.20 Registration-offering 37
3.3.21 TokenizerController 40
3.3.22 Credential 41
3.3.23 Issuer 41

4 Deployment Guides   **43**
4.1   Artifact Deployment Guides 43
4.2   MDS1: Manual Deployment 44
4.3   ADS1: Automatized Deployment with Ansible Scenario One   45
4.4   ADS2: Automated Deployment with Ansible and CI/CD
      GitHub Pipelines Two 46
4.5   ADS3: Automated Deployment with Docker Compose . . . 47
4.6   Tagging Releases Strategy 50
4.7   Deployment Process 50
      4.7.1   Docker Compose 51
      4.7.2   Technical Requirements 52
      4.7.3   Specification and configurations 53
      4.7.4   Deployment 54

5 Operative Specification   **57**
5.1   Libraries 57
5.2   i3-MARKET APIs 58
5.3   SDKs 62
5.4   User Interfaces 63
5.5   Install i3M Wallet 64
5.6   Create a Wallet and a Consumer and/or Provider Identity in
      the Wallet 65
5.7   Creating a Wallet 2/3 66
5.8   Register a New OIDC Client 66
5.9   SDKs 74

6 SDKs and WEB-RI   **79**
6.1   Approach 79

6.2 SDK-Core Specification 80
    6.2.1 SDK-core implementation 82
    6.2.2 Core technology 82
6.3 SDK Reference Implementation (SDK-RI) 85
6.4 WEB-RI 90
    6.4.1 Purpose 90
6.5 IMPLEMENTATION 92
6.6 Navigation: 95

7 Deployment Tools   **103**
7.1 Solution Design 103
    7.1.1 MDS1: manual deployment 105
    7.1.2 ADS1: automated deployment with Ansible 106
    7.1.3 ADS2: automated deployment with Ansible and
           CI/CD GitHub pipelines 107
    7.1.4 ADS3: automated deployment with Docker Compose 108
7.2 i3-MARKET: Onboarding Process 110

8 SDK-RI Specification   **113**
8.1 Objectives 113
8.2 Technical Requirements 113
8.3 SDK Reference Implementation 113
8.4 Core Technology 114
8.5 Continuous Integration and Deployment 114

9 SDK-RI Installation using Docker   **117**
9.1 Setup 118
9.2 Running the SDK-RI with Docker 118
9.3 Configuring and using SDK-RI 118

10 WEB-RI   **121**
10.1 Purpose 121
10.2 Architecture 121
10.3 Sitemap 123
10.4 Run WEB-RI in Docker 124

11 Central Administration Guide   **125**
11.1 Cloud Management 125
11.2 Infrastructure Monitoring 126

12 Repositories and Open Source   **129**
  12.1 GitLab/GitHub 131
  12.2 GitLab Repository 132
  12.3 GitHub Repository 132
  12.4 Developers' portal with MKDocs framework 133
  12.5 Open-Source Portal 134
      12.5.1 Developers, users, and respective roles 136
      12.5.2 Roles and activities of developers and experts in the
              governance model 137

13 Other Content   **139**
  13.1 Local Development using Node.js 139
  13.2 Local Development using Docker 140
      13.2.1 Development scripts in the docker container 140

14 Conclusions   **141**

References   **145**

Index   **151**

About the Editors   **153**

Preface

Data is the oil in today's global economy. The vision in the i3-MARKET book series is that the fast-growing data marketplaces sector will mature, with a large number of data-driven opportunities for commercialization and activating new innovation channels for the data.

A new data-as-a-service paradigm where the data can be traded and commercialized securely and transparently and with total liberty at the local and global scale directly from the data producer is necessary. This new paradigm is the result of an evolution process where data producers are more active owners of the collected data while at the same time catapulting disruptive data-centric applications and services. i3-MARKET takes a step forward and provides support tools for this maturity vision/process.

i3-MARKET is a fully open-source backplane platform that can be used as a set of support tools or a standalone platform implementation of data economy support services. i3-MARKET is the result of shared perspectives from a representative global group of experts, providing a common vision in data economy and identifying impacts and business opportunities in the different areas where data is produced.

Data economy is commonly referring to the diversity in the use of data to provide social benefits and have a direct impact in people's life. From a technological point of view, data economy implies technological services to underpin the delivery of data applications that bring value and address the diverse demands on selling, buying, and trading data assets. The demand and the supply side in the data is increasing exponentially, and it is being demonstrated that the value that the data has today is as relevant as any other tangible and intangible assets in the global economy.

This publication is supported with EU research funds under grant agreement i3-MARKET-871754. Intelligent, Interoperable, Integrative and deployable open source MARKETplace with trusted and secure software tools for incentivising the industry data economy and the Science Foundation Ireland research funds under grant agreement SFI/12/RC/2289_P2. Insight SFI Research Centre for Data Analytics. The European Commission and the SFI support for the production of this publication does not constitute an endorsement of the contents, which reflect the views only of the authors, and the Commission, the SFI or its authors cannot be held responsible for any use which may be made of the information contained therein.

Dr. J. Martin Serrano O.
i3-MARKET Scientific Manager and Data Scientist
Adjunct Lecturer and Senior SFI Research Fellow at University of Galway
Data Science Institute - Insight SFI Research Centre for Data Analytics
Unit Head of Internet of Things, Stream Processing and Intelligent Systems
Research Group
University of Galway, www.universityofgalway.ie | Ollscoil na Gaillimh
<jamiemartin.serranoorozco@universityofgalway.ie>
<martin.serrano@insight-centre.org>
<martin.serrano@nuigalway.ie>

i3-MARKET

Who Should Read this Book?

General Public and Students

This Book is a unique opportunity for understanding the future of data spaces and marketplace assets, their services, and their ability to identify different methodologies indicators and the data-driven economy from a human-centric perspective supports the digital transformation.

Entrepreneurs and SMEs

This Book is a unique opportunity for understanding the most updated software tools to innovate, increase opportunities, and increase the power of innovation into small and entrepreneurs to meet its full potential promoting participation across the data economy values and evolution of society towards a single digital strategy.

Technical Experts and Software Developers

This book is a guide for technolgy experts and open source enthusiast that includes the most recent experiences in Europe towards innovating software technology for the financial and banking sectors.

Data Spaces & Data Markeplaces Policy Makers

This Book represent a unique offering for non-technical experts but that participates in the data economy process and the core data economy servicesto enable the sharing of innovation and new services across data spaces and marketplaces such as policy makers and standardisation organisatiosna and groups.

What is Addressed in the i3-MARKET Book Series?

"Concepts and Design Innovations for the Digital Transformation of Spaces and Marketplaces"

In the first part of the i3-MARKET book series, we begin by discussing the principles of the modern data economy that lead to make the society more aware about the value of the data that is being produced everyday by themselves but also in a collective manner, i.e., in an industrial manufacturing plant, a smart city full of sensors generating data about the behaviours of the city and their inhabitants and/or the wellbeing and healthcare levels of a region or specific locations, etc. Data business is one of the most disruptive areas in today's global economy, particularly with the value that large corporates have embedded in their solutions and products as a result of the use of data from every individual.

"Systems and Implemented technologies for Data-driven Innovation, Addressing Data Spaces and Marketplaces Semantic Interoperability Needs"

In the second i3-MARKET series book, we start reviewing the basic technological principles and software best practices and standards for implementing and deploying data spaces and data marketplaces. The book provides a definition for data-driven society as: *The process to transform data production into data economy for the people using the emerging technologies and scientific advances in data science to underpin the delivery of data economic models and services.* This book further discusses why data spaces and data marketplaces are the focus in today's data-driven society as the trend to rapidly transforming the data perception in every aspect of our activities. In this book, technology assets that are designed and implemented following the i3-MARKET backplane reference implementation (WebRI) that uses open data, big data, IoT, and AI design principles are introduced. Moreover, the series of software assets grouped as subsystems and composed by software artefacts are included and explained in full. Further, we describe i3-MARKET backplane tools and how these can be used for supporting marketplaces and its components including details of available data assets. Next, we provide a description of solutions developed in i3-MARKET as an overview of the potential for being the reference open source solution to improve data economy across different data marketplaces.

"Technical Innovation, Solving the Data Spaces and Marketplaces Interoperability Problems for the Global Data-driven Economy"

In the third i3-MARKET series book, we are focusing on including the best practices and simplest software methods and mechanisms that allow the i3-MARKET backplane reference implementation to be instantiated, tested, and validated even before the technical experts and developers community decide to integrate the i3-MARKET as a reference implementation or adopted open source software tools. In this book, the purpose of offering a guide book for technical experts and developers is addressed. This book addresses the so-called industrial deployment or pilots that need to have a clear understanding of the technological components and also the software infrastructures, thus it is important to provide the easy-to-follow steps to avoid overwhelm the deployment process.

i3-MARKET has three industrial pilots defined in terms of data resources used to deploy data-driven applications that use the most of the i3-MARKET backplane services and functionalities. The different software technologies developed, including the use of open source frameworks, within the context of the i3-MARKET are considered as a bill of software artefacts of the resources needed to perform demonstrators, proof of concepts, and prototype solutions. The i3-MARKET handbook provided can actually be used as input for configurators and developers to set up and pre-test testbeds, and, therefore, it is extremely valuable to organizations to be used properly.

What is Covered in this i3-MARKET Part III Book?

"The i3-MARKET FOSS Handbook"

Technology deployment tools, software development frameworks and testbed tools (sandboxes) are popular these days, to facilitate the complexity of deploying applications and services based on complex software packages, from a practical point of view the deployment and testing of software technology should not be an burden anymore as per the large number of technologies that exist but also because the evolution of these software tools is indicating sooner than later this will only relay in having powerful systems capable to run such complex frameworks and the rest is just provide few steps to configure and execute the deployment. The reality is a bit different, while there are excellent tools to deploy and run software virtually everywhere, the technology must run in specific computing infrastructures with well-defined specifications and functionalities.

In this third i3-MARKET series book we are focusing in including the best practices and simplest software methods and mechanisms that allow the i3-MARKET backplane reference implementation to be instantiated, tested and validated even before the technical experts and developers' community decide to integrate the i3-MARKET as a reference implementation or Adopted Open-Source Software tools. At this book the purpose of offering a guidebook for technical experts and developers is addressed, the so-called industrial deployment or pilots need to have clear understanding of the technological components but also the software infrastructures, alike the steps to be followed to avoid overwhelm the deployment activity.

i3-MARKET has three industrial Pilots defined in terms of data resources used to deploy datadriven applications that uses the most of the i3-MARKET backplane services and functionalities. The different software technologies developed, including the use of open-source frameworks, within the context of the i3-MARKET is considered as a bill of software artefacts of the resources needed to perform demonstrators, proof of concepts and prototype solutions. The i3-MARKET handbook provided can actually be used as input for configurators

i3-MARKET

Acknowledgements

Immense thanks to our families for their incomparable affection, jollity, and constant understanding that scientific career is not a work but a lifestyle, for encouraging us to be creative, for their enormous patience during the time away from them, invested in our scientific endeavours and responsibilities, and for their understanding about our deep love to our professional life and its consequences – we love you!

To all our friends and relatives for their comprehension when we had no time to spend with them and when we were not able to join in time because we were in a conference or attending yet another meeting and for their attention and the interest they have been showing all this time to keep our friendship alive; be sure, our sacrifices are well rewarded.

To all our colleagues, staff members, and students at our respective institutions, organizations, and companies for patiently listening with apparent attention to the descriptions and progress of our work and for the great experiences and the great time spent while working together with us and the contributions provided to culminate this book series project. In particular, thanks to the support and confidence from all people who believed this series of books would be finished in time and also to those who did not trust on it, because, thanks to them, we were more motivated to culminate the project.

To the scientific community, who is our family when we are away and working far from our loved ones, for their incomparable affection, loyalty, and constant encouragement to be creative, and for their enormous patience during the time invested in understanding, presenting, and providing feedback to new concepts and ideas – sincerely to you all, thanks a million!

Martín Serrano on Behalf of All Authors

i3-MARKET

List of Figures

Figure 2.1 i3M ecosystem deployment diagram. 9
Figure 2.2 i3M ecosystem deployment diagram. 11
Figure 2.3 i3M SW stack four layers. 12
Figure 2.4 i3M centralized software stack layers. 13
Figure 2.5 i3M pilots' software stack layers. 15
Figure 3.1 Backplane gateway architecture. 20
Figure 3.2 Backplane authentication flow overview. 21
Figure 3.3 Backplane authorization flow overview. 22
Figure 3.4 Service integrator process overview. 25
Figure 3.5 Subsystem OAS automatic integration mechanism
                overview. 26
Figure 3.6 Backplane automatic integration mechanism
                overview. 28
Figure 3.7 Ansible playbook run overview. 29
Figure 3.8 Server election process example. 30
Figure 4.1 MDS1. 44
Figure 4.2 ADS1. 45
Figure 4.3 Ansible playbook example. 46
Figure 4.4 ADS2. 46
Figure 4.5 i3-MARKET CI/CD with Ansible and GitHub. . . . 47
Figure 4.6 Requirement.txt for semantic engine repository. . 51
Figure 5.1 Services and queues common services. 58
Figure 5.2 Alerts common services. 58
Figure 5.3 Conflict resolution common services. 59
Figure 5.4 Contracts common services. 59
Figure 5.5 Contracts common services. 60

Figure 5.6   Exchange common services.   60
Figure 5.7   Notification common services.   60
Figure 5.8   Offering common services.   61
Figure 5.9   Pricing common services.   62
Figure 5.10   Tokens common services.   62
Figure 5.11   Implementation pyramid.   64
Figure 5.12   Creating a wallet 1/3.   65
Figure 5.13   WEB-RI interface.   66
Figure 5.14   Creating a wallet 3/3.   66
Figure 5.15   OIDC client configuration.   67
Figure 5.16   Registering an OIDC Client 1/4.   67
Figure 5.17   Registering an OIDC client 2/4.   68
Figure 5.18   Registering an OIDC client 3/4.   68
Figure 5.19   Registering an OIDC client 4/4.   69
Figure 5.20   OIDC client registered.   69
Figure 5.21   Username screen.   70
Figure 5.22   Pairing wallet.   70
Figure 5.23   Configuring wallet 1/2.   71
Figure 5.24   Configuring wallet 2/2.   71
Figure 5.25   Login in WEB-RI.   72
Figure 5.26   Selective disclosure.   72
Figure 5.27   Signing with the wallet.   73
Figure 5.28   Accessing WEB-RI.   73
Figure 5.29   SDK-generator approach.   75
Figure 5.30   SDK generator supported programming languages.   76
Figure 5.31   SDK-core CI/CD pipeline.   76
Figure 6.1   SDK layered approach.   80
Figure 6.2   SDK-core interactions.   81
Figure 6.3   SDK-generator approach.   83
Figure 6.4   SDK-generator supported programming
                    languages.   83
Figure 6.5   SDK-core CI/CD pipeline.   84
Figure 6.6   SDK-core playbook internal workflow.   84
Figure 6.7   Services and queues common services.   85
Figure 6.8   Alerts common services.   86
Figure 6.9   Conflict resolution common services.   86
Figure 6.10   Contracts common services.   86
Figure 6.11   Credentials common services.   87
Figure 6.12   Exchange common services.   87

Figure 6.13	Notification common services.	87
Figure 6.14	Offering common services.	88
Figure 6.15	Pricing common services.	89
Figure 6.16	Token common services.	89
Figure 6.17	WEB-RI architecture.	91
Figure 6.18	WEB-RI sitemap.	92
Figure 6.19	WEB-RI registration page.	93
Figure 6.20	WEB-RI register with wallet.	94
Figure 6.21	WEB-RI login page.	94
Figure 6.22	WEB-RI login with wallet.	95
Figure 6.23	WEB-RI navigation (provider).	95
Figure 6.24	WEB-RI navigation (consumer).	96
Figure 6.25	WEB-RI home page.	96
Figure 6.26	WEB-RI offerings page.	97
Figure 6.27	WEB-RI offering details page.	98
Figure 6.28	WEB-RI offering registration page.	99
Figure 6.29	WEB-RI offering purchase page.	100
Figure 6.30	WEB-RI search page.	101
Figure 6.31	WEB-RI notifications page.	102
Figure 7.1	Four-layer i3M SW stack.	104
Figure 7.2	MDS1.	105
Figure 7.3	ADS1.	106
Figure 7.4	Ansible playbook example.	107
Figure 7.5	ADS2.	107
Figure 7.6	CI/CD with Ansible and GitHub.	108
Figure 8.1	SDK-RI Implementation Technologies Used. . . .	114
Figure 8.2	SDK-RI pipeline based on Ansible AWX.	115
Figure 8.3	SDK-core/RI playbook internal workflow.	116
Figure 10.1	WEB-RI architecture.	122
Figure 10.2	WEB-RI sitemap.	123
Figure 11.1	Ansible Tower dashboard view.	125
Figure 11.2	Ansible resource inventory definition view.	126
Figure 11.3	Ansible Tower metrics data flow.	127
Figure 11.4	i3-MARKET Zabbix instance.	128
Figure 12.1	Open-source developers portal with MKDocs. . .	134
Figure 12.2	Code repository.	134
Figure 12.3	Open-source governance.	135
Figure 12.4	Public repository governance.	137

i3-MARKET

List of Tables

Table 2.1   i3M proprietary conceptual artifacts.   7
Table 2.2   i3M centralized cloud management and monitoring
            software.   13
Table 2.3   i3M centralized DevOps software.   14
Table 2.4   i3M centralized third-party software.   14
Table 2.5   I3M centralized proprietary software.   15
Table 2.6   i3M pilots' core artifacts.   16
Table 2.7   i3M pilots' third-party artifacts.   17
Table 4.1   Deployment scenarios and i3M user roles mapping. .   44
Table 4.2   i3m-pilots-docker-compose.yml.   48
Table 7.1   Deployment scenarios and i3M user roles mapping. .   105

List of Contributors

Achille, Zappa, *NUIG, Ireland*

Alessandro, Amicone, *GFT, Italy*

Andrei, Coman, *Siemens SRL, Romania*

Andres, Ojamaa, *Guardtime, Estonia*

Angel, Cataron, *Siemens SRL, Romania*

Antonio, Jara, *Libellium/HOPU, Spain*

Birthe, Boehm, *Siemens AG (Erlangen), Germany*

Borja, Ruiz, *Atos, Spain*

Bruno, Almeida, *UNPARALLEL, Portugal*

Bruno, Michel, *IBM, Switzerland*

Carlos Miguel, Pina Vaz Gomes, *IBM, Switzerland*

Carmen, Pereira, *Atos, Spain*

Chi, Hung Le, *NUIG, Ireland*

Deborah, Goll, *Digital SME, Belgium*

Dimitris, Drakoulis, *Telesto, Greece*

Edgar, Fries, *Siemens AG (Erlangen), Germany*

Fernando, Román García, *UPC, Spain*

Filia, Filippou, *Telesto, Greece*

George, Benos, *Telesto, Greece*

German, Molina, *Libellium/HOPU, Spain*

Hoan, Quoc, *NUIG, Ireland*

Iosif, Furtuna, *Siemens SRL, Romania*

Isabelle, Landreau, *IDEMIA, France*

Ivan, Martinez, *Atos, Spain*

James, Philpot, *Digital SME, Belgium*

Jean Loup, Depinay, *IDEMIA, France*

Joao, Oliveira, *UNPARALLEL, Portugal*

Jose, Luis Muñoz Tapia, *UPC, Spain*

Juan Eleazar, Escudero, *Libellium/HOPU, Spain*

Juan, Hernández Serrano, *UPC, Spain*

Juan , Salmerón, *UPC, Spain*

Justina, Bieliauskaite, *Digital SME, Belgium*

Kaarel, Hanson, *Guardtime, Estonia*

Lauren, Del Giudice, *IDEMIA, France*

Luca, Marangoni, *GFT, Italy*

Lucas, Asmelash, *Digital SME, Belgium*

Lukas, Zimmerli, *IBM, Switzerland*

Márcio, Mateus, *UNPARALLEL, Portugal*

Marc, Catrisse, *UPC, Spain*

Mari, Paz Linares, *UPC, Spain*

Maria Angeles, Sanguino Gonzalez, *Atos, Spain*

Maria, Smyth, *NUIG, Ireland*

Marina, Cugurra, *ETA Consulting*

Marquart, Franz, *Siemens AG (Munich), Germany*

Martin, Serrano, *NUIG, Ireland*

Mirza, Fardeen Baig, *NUIG, Ireland*

Oxana, Matruglio, *Siemens AG (Munich), Germany*

Pascal, Duville, *IDEMIA, France*

Pedro, Ferreira, *UNPARALLEL, Portugal*

Pedro, Malo, *UNPARALLEL, Portugal*

Philippe, Hercelin, *IDEMIA, France*

Qaiser, Mehmood, *NUIG, Ireland*

Rafael, Genés, *UPC, Spain*

Raul, Santos, *Atos, Spain*

Rishabh, Chandaliya, *NUIG, Ireland*

Rupert, Gobber, *GFT, Italy*

Stefanie, Wolf, *Siemens AG(Erlangen), Germany*

Stratos, Baloutsos, *AUEB, Greece*

Susanne, Stahnke, *Siemens AG (Munich), Germany*

Tanel, Ojalill, *Guardtime, Estonia*

Timoleon, Farmakis, *AUEB, Greece*

Tomas, Pariente Lobo, *Atos, Spain*

Toufik, Ailane, *Siemens AG (Erlangen), Germany*

Víctor, Diví, *UPC, Spain*

Vasiliki, Koniakou, *AUEB, Greece*

Yvonne, Kovacs, *Siemens SRL, Romania*

i3-MARKET

List of Abbreviations

AI	Artificial intelligence
API	Application program interface
APP	Mobile application/web application
CA	Certificate authority
CSMT	Compact sparse merkle tree
DB	Data base
DCAT	Data catalog vocabulary
DID	Decentralized identifier
DLT	Distributed ledger technology
DSA	Data sharing agreement
ECDSA	Elliptic curve digital signature algorithm
HMAC	Hash-based message authentication code
IAM	Identity and access management
IDM	Identity management
IoT	Internet of things
IRI	Information reuse and integration
JWT	JSON web token
KOS	Knowledge organization system
NAL	Nexus authorization logic
O-CASUS	Ontology for control, access, save, use and security
OIDC	OpenID connect
OSS	Open source software
PAV	Privacy, anonymity, and verifiability
PDU	Protocol data unit
PoO	Proof of origin

PoP	Proof of publication
PoR	Proof of reception
QoS	Quality of service
RP	Relying party
RSA	Rivest-Shamir-Adleman cryptosystem
SDA	Secure data access
SDK	Software development kit
SKOS	Simple knowledge organization system
SLA	Service level agreement
SLS	Service level specification
SME	Small and medium-sized enterprises
SQL	Structured query language
SSI	Self-sovereign identity
TLS	Transport layer security
URI	Uniform resource identifier
VC	Verifiable credentials
VDI	Verifiable database integrity
VoID	Vocabulary of interlinked datasets

1

---

i3-MARKET Overview

The i3-MARKET project (i3-market.eu) solutions address the growing demand for a single European Data Market and Data Economy.

i3-MARKET addresses the data economy challenge by innovating marketplace platforms, demonstrating with industrial implementations that the data economy growth is possible. The i3-MARKET solutions aim at providing technologies for trustworthy (secure and reliable), data-driven collaboration and federation of existing and new future marketplace platforms, with special attention on industrial data. The i3-MARKET architecture is designed to enable secure and privacy-preserving data sharing across data spaces and marketplaces, through the deployment of a Backplane across operational data marketplaces.

In i3-MARKET, we are not trying to create another new Marketplace, but we are implementing the Backplane solutions that allow other data marketplaces and data spaces to expand their market, facilitate the registration and discovery of data assets, facilitate the trading and sharing of data assets among providers, consumers, and owners, and provide tools to add functionalities they lack for better data sharing and trading processes.

The i3-MARKET project has built a blueprint open-source software architecture called "i3-MARKET Backplane" (www.open-source.i3-MARKET.eu) that addresses the growing demand for connecting multiple data spaces and marketplaces in a secure and federated manner.

The i3-MARKET Consortium is contributing with the developed software tools to build the European Data Market Economy by innovating marketplace platforms, and demonstrating with three industrial reference implementations (pilots) that a decentralized data economy and more fair growth is possible.

1.1 Context

A software deployment guide is a document that outlines the process and best practices for deploying software to a production environment. It is an essential resource for developers, system administrators, and operations teams who are responsible for deploying software in a reliable and efficient manner.

Overall, a well-written software deployment guide is an invaluable resource for ensuring that software is deployed in a reliable and efficient manner. By following best practices and established procedures, organizations can minimize the risk of downtime and ensure that their software is delivering the intended benefits to end-users.

2

General Description

i3-MARKET leverages on blockchain technologies (e.g. Hyperledger and Ethereum) to build a trusted, interoperable, and decentralized substrate (backplane) allowing to create a federated data market where data spaces and marketplaces are able to trade data assets among each other. The i3-MARKET is mostly a set of independent subsystems with a self-contained functionality such as the identity and access management system, the semantic engine subsystem, data access subsystem, etc. Most of these subsystems have broken down their functionality into atomic and loosely coupled components exposing their functionality through a REST API, which yields a microservice-based nature to the i3-MARKET system

2.1 Deployment and Operational Concepts

Help to choose the right technologies to be used:
Choosing the right technologies for software deployments can be a complex process, but here are some general guidelines to help you make informed decisions:

2.1.1 Consider the requirements of the software

The first step in choosing the right technologies for a deployment is to consider the requirements of the software being deployed. This includes factors such as the operating system, the programming language used, the database management system, and any dependencies or third-party libraries required.

2.1.2 Evaluate the deployment environment

The deployment environment will also play a key role in determining the appropriate technologies to be used. Consider factors such as the hardware

3

and software infrastructure, the network configuration, and the security requirements.

2.1.3 Consider automation and orchestration

Automation and orchestration tools can help to streamline the deployment process and minimize the risk of errors or inconsistencies. Consider using tools such as Ansible, Chef, or Puppet to automate the deployment process.

2.1.4 Evaluate containerization options

Containerization technologies such as Docker and Kubernetes can help to simplify the deployment process and make it more portable across different environments. Consider using containerization technologies to deploy software in a consistent and repeatable way.

2.1.5 Consider monitoring and reporting tools

Monitoring and reporting tools can help to ensure that the software is performing as expected and can alert teams to potential issues before they become critical. Consider using tools such as Nagios, Prometheus, or Grafana to monitor and report on key metrics.

2.2 Deployment Specification

The i3-MARKET architecture specification is based on the 4 + 1 architectural view model approach. One of these views, physical view, is the scope of this document. Physical view depicts the system from a system engineer's point of view. It concerns the topology of software components on the physical layer as well as the physical connections between these components. This view is also known as the deployment view. UML diagrams used to represent the physical view must include the deployment diagram.

Considering this in the i3-MARKET context, the deployment specification should define execution architecture of systems that represent the assignment (deployment) of software artifacts (i3-MARKET building blocks) to deployment targets (usually nodes).

Nodes represent either hardware devices or software execution environments. They could be connected through communication paths to create network systems of arbitrary complexity. Artifacts represent concrete elements in the physical architecture.

Once the deployment has been provided, a complementary specification would be necessary to define how to deploy software within the i3-MARKET ecosystem. In the context of i3-MARKET, we will be referring to this specification as management operative specification.

Finally, an end-user operative specification is provided, defining the interaction with i3-MARKET from a stakeholder point of view.

2.3 Terminology

The key terms behind i3-MARKET deployment terminology are the following:

Artifact:

As it is described in [1], an artifact is a classifier that represents some physical entity, a piece of information that is used or is produced by a software development process, or by deployment and operation of a system. Artifact is a source of a deployment to a node. A particular instance (or "copy") of an artifact is deployed to a node instance. The most common artifacts are as follows:

- Source files
- Executable files
- Database tables
- Scripts
- DLL files
- User manuals or documentation
- Output files

Artifacts are deployed on the nodes. They can provide physical manifestation for any UML element. Generally, they manifest components. Artifacts are labelled with the stereotype <<artifact>>, and it may have an artifact icon on the top right corner.

Each artifact has a filename in its specification that indicates the physical location of the artifact. An artifact can contain another artifact. It may be dependent on one another.

Artifacts have properties and behaviour that manipulate them.

Node:

As it is introduced in [2], a node is a computational resource upon which artifacts are deployed for execution. A node is a physical thing that can execute one or more artifacts. A node may vary in its size depending on the size of the project.

Node is an essential UML element that describes the execution of code and the communication between various entities of a system. It is denoted by a 3D box with the node name written inside of it. Nodes help to convey the hardware that is used to deploy the software.

An association between nodes represents a communication path from which information is exchanged in any direction.

Generally, a node has two stereotypes as follows:

- $<<$ **device** $>>$: It is a node that represents a physical machine capable of performing computations. A device can be a router or a server PC. It is represented using a node with stereotype $<<$device$>>$. In the UML model, you can also nest one or more devices within each other.
- $<<$ **execution environment** $>>$: It is a node that represents an environment in which software is going to execute. For example, Java applications are executed in Java virtual machine (JVM). JVM is considered as an execution environment for Java applications. We can nest an execution environment into a device node. You can nest more than one execution environments in a single device node.

The following sections report on the deployment strategy and the status reached at the closure of the final release.

2.4 i3-MARKET Artifacts Overview

In the context of i3-MARKET, several artifacts have been developed, integrated, and deployed. These artifacts have been built on top of a set of third-party and open-source frameworks, which have been analysed and deployed as tech-bed for the construction of the i3-MARKET backplane. For the final release, the third-party artifacts included on i3-MARKET are:

- Hyperledger Besu: The blockchain framework.
- CockroachDB: Distributed database deployed on each node. Admin Interface only accessible through node 1.
- RocksDB: Decentralized storage included with the blockchain network (ledger).
- Loopback4: Framework supporting i3-MARKET backplane API.

Regarding the project-internal conceptual artifacts, i3-MARKET has developed an extensive artifacts portfolio, mainly provided in WP3 and WP4, for supporting the integration, registration, discovery, and transfer of reliable trade of data. A detailed list of these artifacts (including artifact ID, artifact name, artifact dependencies, and their status for the final release) can be seen in Table 2.1.

Table 2.1 i3M proprietary conceptual artifacts.

Artifact ID	Artifact	Dependencies	Final release use	Notes
A1	Blockchain framework	Decentralized storage	Deployed and used	Blockchain framework. Deployed on each node.
A2	CockroachDB (distributed storage)		Deployed and used	Distributed database deployed on each node.
A3	Decentralized storage	Blockchain framework	Deployed and used	Included with the blockchain framework.
A4	User-centric authentication		Deployed and used	Each instance/pilot has its own OIDC and VC service.
A5	Service-centric authentication		Deployed and used	Each instance/pilot has its own Keycloak service.
A6	HW Wallet		In progress	
A7	Software Wallet	Cloud Wallet Client, Backplane API (Cloud Wallet server and user-centric authentication), data access SDK, and i3-MARKET SDK	Deployed and used	
A8	Smart contract manager	SLA/SLE smart contract	Deployed and used	
A9	SLA/SLE smart contract		Deployed and used	
A10	Conflict resolution	SCM and DS	Deployed and used	Integrated with Besu, smart contract manager and decentralized storage. Each instance/pilot has its own service.
A11	Explicit user consent	Backplane API (smart contract manager, distributed ledger, and distributed storage)	Deployed and used	Integrated with the smart contract manager.
A12	Auditable accounting		Deployed and used	
A13	Standard payment	Backplane API (auditable accounting, conflict resolution, smart contract, and SLA/SLE smart contract)	Deployed and used	Library to be integrated and deployed in data access SDK and data access API. Library for the i3-MARKET non-repudiation protocol that helps generate/verifying the necessary proofs and the received block of data.
A14	Tokenization	Backplane API (user-centric authentication, smart contract, and SLA/SLE smart contract)	Deployed and used	

Table 2.1   *Continued.*

Artifact ID	Artifact	Dependencies	Final release use	Notes
A15	Micro payment		Deployed	Integrated into the Tokenizer. Low chance to be used by i3-MARKET because for data payments is used fiat money and the Tokenizer and the token are just for the fees.
A17	Data access API		Deployed and used	Each node has its own endpoint.
A18	Semantic data manager (triple store)		Deployed and used	
A19	Semantic models		Deployed and used	It is not software component.
A20	Semantic engine	Backplane API (user IDs) and decentralized storage	Deployed and used	This component includes - Semantic model management - Offering and discovery Each instance/pilot has their own engine
A21	Backplane API	All	Deployed and used	Each node has its own endpoint
A22	i3-MARKET SDK-generator		Deployed and used	Endpoint at node 1 Deployed as Docker container through Ansible
A26	SDK-RI (reference implementation)	All	Deployed and used	Each marketplace has its own SDK-RI
A27	SDK-core	SDK-generatore All	Deployed and used	Available at Nexus
A29	Secure server (Keycloak)		Deployed	Available at Nexus Integration with user-centric authentication component in progress
A30	Notification manager	SDK-RI and SDK-core	Deployed and used	
A31	Rating		Deployed and used	

Finally, in the context of CI/CD, a set of tools has been used for the automation and monitoring of the artifacts deployed on i3-MARKET. These tools are listed in the deliverable D4.7 and in the sections below.

2.5 Deployment Architecture View

The i3-MARKET deployment view is depicted in the picture below. Four nodes constituted the i3-MARKET R1 cluster. On each node, it will be deployed a Backplane gateway system and an instance of all the rest i3-MARKET main building blocks (trust, security, and privacy system, storage system, and data access system) giving backend support to the Backplane gateway system. In addition to that, node 4 will host all the components related with the semantic engine building block.

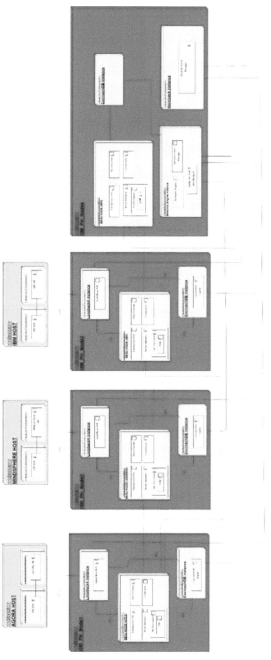

Figure 2.1   i3M ecosystem deployment diagram.

2.6 i3-MARKET Network Infrastructure

Figure 2.1 shows the deployment diagram associated with the i3-MARKET network for the last release. It can be appreciated that the deployment strategy has evolved from the M18 centralized infrastructure (where a single and centralized i3-MARKET instance gave support to all demonstrators) to a "hybrid" decentralized infrastructure (where each of the pilot's demonstrator that joined the i3-MARKET ecosystem has its own i3-MARKET instance). It is important to highlight the "hybrid" nature of the network because a master instance is maintaining, among other reasons, some centralized services such as the central Besu node, the notification manager, etc., and CI/CD tools needed for the setup of the network.

Therefore, in this landscape, it can be appreciated the existence of marketplaces, which are simple instances (yellow boxes) and the central/master instances (green boxes). The most significant relationship among the instances is the connection between each of the Besu nodes themselves and their connection with the Besu central node.

It is important to mention that the number of nodes used for each of the i3-MARKET pilot instances and the maintenance of these nodes is up to the pilots' criteria and responsibility. Thus, the node's layout that appears on each of the instances, depicted for hosting the i3-MARKET artifacts, Figures 2.1 and 2.2, is just an example and does not have to be the real picture of the instances deployment.

2.7 Software Stack

For the final release, two types of software environments (understood as a set of artifacts) can be found in i3-MARKET, which are aligned with the infrastructures presented in the previous section. On one hand, the marketplace-side software stack (i3-MARKET pilot environment) and, on the other hand, the stack landscape deployed in the centralized cluster (i3-MARKET master environment), which acts as a master for the rest of marketplaces, adhere to the i3-MARKET network.

A four-layer stack has been defined for i3-MARKET (Figure 2.3): at the lowest layer, there is the Cloud provisioning and management layer. On top of that, a DevOps software layer is placed for assembling all the software used for the CI/CD process. Then, a third-party software layer is in charge of giving support to the i3M Core Artifacts, which can be found at the top level of the stack.

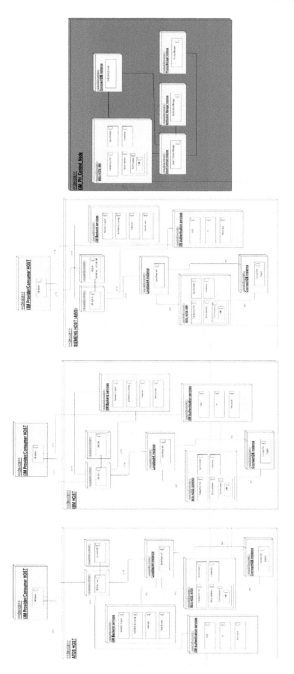

Figure 2.2 i3M ecosystem deployment diagram.

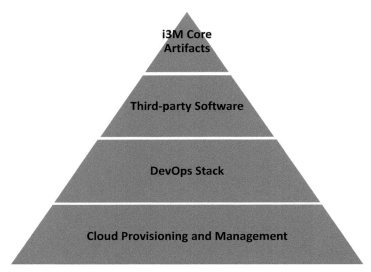

Figure 2.3   i3M SW stack four layers.

Depending on the environment to be deployed, it might deploy one layer or another. More details on the specific software deployed on each environment are given in the following sub-sections.

2.8 i3-MARKET Master Environment

The i3-MARKET centralized software stack, represented in Figure 2.4, is focused on providing the minimum and centralized services for erecting an i3-MARKET network; these are the "Cloud provisioning and management" layer, the "DevOps software" layer, master nodes of the "Third-party software" layer, and the centralized i3-MARKET artifacts provided in the "i3M centralized services" layer.

Cloud provisioning and management layer oversees providing and managing all physical nodes that the i3-MARKET common infrastructure is composed of. For the management of physical resources in a homogeneous way, an Ansible Tower[1] instance is deployed for the administration of said physical resources, thus having their management centralized from Ansible. On the other hand, for the monitoring and registering of the status of the i3-MARKET central services, Zabbix is deployed as part of the central

---

[1] Ansible Tower: https://www.ansible.com/products/tower

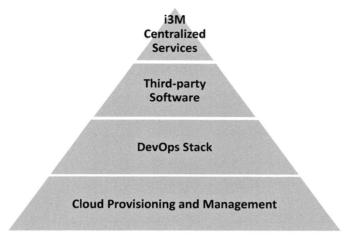

Figure 2.4 i3M centralized software stack layers.

environment. Table 2.2 shows some deployment aspects of the previously commented tools:

Table 2.2 i3M centralized cloud management and monitoring software.

SW Component	Building block	Assigned VM/PR	Type	Technology
Ansible AWX	Deployment	I3M-PH-Node2	Third-party SW	Ansible AWX
Zabbix	Monitoring	I3M-PH-Node4	Third-party SW	Zabbix

i3-MARKET DevOps will be a set of practices that will combine software development and IT operations, and it will aim to shorten the i3-MARKET system development life cycle and provide continuous delivery with high software quality. Thus, the DevOps layer combines software development and IT operations by means of the artifacts listed in Table 2.3.

Besides that, a set of artifacts from the i3-MARKET third-party software is needed in the centralized environment to master some services:

- Master Besu node, which gives authorization to new member to the blockchain network.
- Cockroach data base, which hosts the "Seed Index" for federating queries.
- RocksDB, which is the central instance of the blockchain.
- Security services for allowing authentication and authorization capabilities to the central node.

Table 2.3 i3M centralized DevOps software.

SW Component	Building block	Assigned VM/PR	Type	Technology
Ansible AWX	Deployment	I3M-PH-Node2	Third-party SW	Ansible AWX
Docker Swarm	Deployment	I3M-PH-Node1, I3M-PH-Node2, I3M-PH-Node3, and I3M-PH-Node4	Third-party SW	Docker Swarm
GitLab CI/CD (Runners)	CI/CD	GitLab (out of i3M cluster)	Third-party SW	GitLab
Nexus	CI/CD	I3M-PH-Node4	Third-party SW	Nexus
NGINX	Management/security	I3M-PH-Node1, I3M-PH-Node2, I3M-PH-Node3, and I3M-PH-Node4	Third-party SW	NGinx
MkDocs	Documentation	I3M-PH-Node4	Third-party SW	MkDocs

Table 2.4 shows some deployment details regarding the before commented artifacts.

Table 2.4 i3M centralized third-party software.

SW Component	Building block	Assigned VM/PR	Type	Technology
Blockchain framework (central node)	Blockchain network	I3M-PH-Node4	Third-party SW	Hyperledger Besu
Distributed storage	Data storage	I3M-PH-Node4	Third-party SW	CockroachDB
Decentralized storage	Data storage	I3M-PH-Node4	Third-party SW	RocksDB
Security server	Trust, security, and privacy	I3M-PH-Node4	Third-party SW	OIDC, VC, and Keycloak

Finally, regarding the "i3-MARKET centralized services", the notification manager and the SDK-generator (which support the SDK-core generator) have been designed to be centralized. Table 2.5 shows some deployment details of them.

Table 2.5 I3M centralized proprietary software.

SW Component	Building block	Assigned VM/PR	Type	Technology
Notification manager	Data storage	I3M-PH-Node4	i3-MARKET SW	RabittMQ
SDK-generator	Reference implementation	I3M-PH-Node4	Hybrid artifact	OpenAPI Generator[2]

2.9 i3-MARKET Pilot Environment

The i3-MARKET pilots' stack is represented in Figure 2.5 and it is composed mainly of two layers: "Third-party software" layer and "i3M core services" layer.

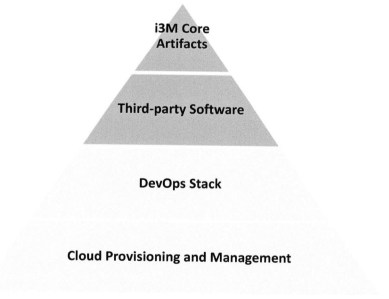

Figure 2.5 i3M pilots' software stack layers.

The top layer is composed of all i3-MARKET core artifacts supplied by the project, which might be deployed in a decentralized way. In other words, each marketplace willing to be part of the i3-MARKET ecosystem might have one instance of these artifacts running on its own i3-MARKET infrastructure. Table 2.6 shows more information about these artifacts/components as well as the set of services provided by each of them (linked with the Microservices View in D2.4). Other details that can be found in the table are:

- SW artifact/component name
- Associated building block (see internal deliverable I2.41 [3])
- Artifact type
- Technology supporting artifact

Table 2.6 i3M pilots' core artifacts.

SW Component	Building block	Services	Type	Technology
User-centric authentication	Trust, security, and privacy	Verifiable Credential API	i3-MARKET SW	Keycloak
Service-centric Authentication	Trust, security, and privacy	OIDC provider API	i3-MARKET SW	
Cloud Wallet	Trust, security, and privacy	Wallet Cloud Server and Wallet APP	i3-MARKET SW	
HW Wallet	Trust, security, and privacy		i3-MARKET SW	
Smart contract manager	Trust, security, and privacy	Smart contract manager API + explicit user consent	i3-MARKET SW	Hyperledger Besu, Solidity
Conflict resolution	Trust, security, and privacy	Conflict resolution API	i3-MARKET SW	
Auditable accounting	Trust, security, and privacy	Auditable accounting API	i3-MARKET SW	
Monetization	Trust, security, and privacy	Pricing manager API, Tokenizer API, and non-repudiation protocol library	i3-MARKET SW	
Data access	Data access	Data access API, standard payments system, and data transfer	i3-MARKET SW	

Table 2.6 *Continued.*

SW Component	Building block	Services	Type	Technology
Semantic	Semantics	Semantic engine API (metadata registry management, data offerings, and federated query discovery)	i3-MARKET SW	MongoDB
Backplane API	Backplane		i3-MARKET SW	LoopBack4
SDK-RI	Reference implementation		i3-MARKET SW	Java
Web-RI	Reference implementation		i3-MARKET SW	

Finally, the "Third-party SW" layer will be mainly in charge of providing the software stack identified as software requirements by the i3-MARKET system. These software requirements are: Hyperledger Besu, CockroachDB, Loopback4, and Keycloak. The Table 2.7 summarise the i3M pilot third party artifacts used.

Table 2.7 i3M pilots' third-party artifacts.

SW Component	Building block	Type	Technology
Blockchain framework	Blockchain network	Third-party SW	Hyperledger Besu
Distributed storage	Data storage	Third-party SW	CockroachDB (deployed standalone)
Decentralized storage	Data storage	Third-party SW	RocksDB
Security server	Trust, security, and privacy	Third-party SW	Keycloak

Regarding "DevOps Stack" and "Cloud provisioning and management", these two layers are out of scope of the stack provided by i3-MARKET on each external instance. This is mainly because of two reasons:

- Each pilot is responsible for deciding, deploying, and using the nodes management and service monitoring tools most suitable to its needs and restrictions. Thus, for example, IBM pilot has decided to use Trivy[3] for scanning vulnerabilities in the deployment of its i3-MARKET instance.

- As it was commented in the infrastructure sections, self-management by the pilot is assumed where to deploy each artifact. Therefore the "Cloud provisioning and management" layer is now under the scope of the pilot administrators.

---

[3] https://www.aquasec.com/products/trivy/

3

Backplane API Gateway

3.1 Objectives

The Backplane gateway system is the building block in charge of offering to all participants and marketplaces access to the Backplane system. The goal of the Backplane API is therefore twofold: on the one hand, it serves an integrated API endpoint for all the i3-MARKET services offered by i3-MARKET and implemented in the respective building blocks. On the other hand, it provides secure mechanisms for preventing not-allowed accesses.

In terms of internal connections with other i3-MARKET building blocks, Backplane gateway system has secure communication with the rest of subsystems to integrate their services into the Backplane API, in order to provide secure access to authorized clients.

The Backplane API is the set of endpoints exposed by the gateway. It comprises all the publicly available endpoints of the subsystems integrated with the Backplane, as well as a few other endpoints, belonging to the Backplane itself, used in the authentication/authorization flows.

The API follows the OpenApi Specification 3.0[1]. Furthermore, the endpoints corresponding to each subsystem are generated automatically based on the subsystem's own OpenApi specification, using the *service integrator engine*, written in Dart.

In Figure 3.1, there is an overview of the overall Backplane gateway architecture. It shows how the Backplane router incorporates all subsystem endpoints; so it can redirect each query to the corresponding subsystem, applying an authentication layer above to avoid unauthorized requests. Users can access to the Backplane gateway via the Backplane API, which publishes all available subsystems together with their endpoints, being totally agnostic of its implementation and how to access the subsystem directly.

---

[1]https://swagger.io/specification/

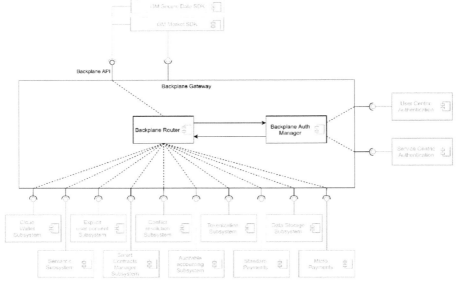

Figure 3.1   Backplane gateway architecture.

The Backplane gateway exposes all subsystem endpoints through a single Backplane API. This simplifies the user interaction with the system; furthermore, it provides an auto-generated documentation that follows the OpenApi specification (OAS).

3.2 Solution Design/Blocks

3.2.1 Authentication and authorization

In the current Backplane API gateway implementation, OAuth 2.0[2] authentication flow is used. Combined together with OpenID Connect (OIDC)[3], that provides a simple identity layer on top. Using OAuth Authorization Code flow (see Figure 3.2), a JWT token is generated at the end of the login flow, which, later, can be used in subsequent queries to authenticate clients against subsystem endpoints, using the Backplane API as gateway.

---

[2]https://oauth.net/2/
[3]https://openid.net/connect/

3.2.1.1 Authentication

Clients are expected to request their JWT token through a given login endpoint, to further request secured endpoints using those credentials.

Thanks to the OpenID Connect identity layer, scopes and claims can be used. Each endpoint can declare a set of scopes, which will be later used to ensure that the requesting user has enough privileges, in a claim-based authorization fashion.

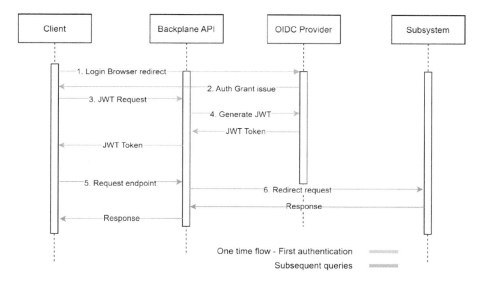

Figure 3.2 Backplane authentication flow overview.

There is a description of each connection considered during the authentication flow described in Figure 3.2:

1. **Login browser redirect:** When a user requests a Backplane authenticated endpoint without providing the required credentials, it is redirected to the identity provider authorization page (OIDC provider).
2. **Auth grant issue:** In case login succeeds, an authorization grant is issued and provided to the client.
3. **JWT request:** The client requests an access token, providing the Auth grant code.
4. **Generate JWT:** Now, the Backplane generates an access token JWT, adding the user claims that are requested to our identity provider.

5. **Request endpoint:** The client uses the previously generated JWT to authenticate their requests to the Backplane.
6. **Redirect request:** In case the user has enough privileges to access the requested endpoint, checking the endpoint scope and user claims, the Backplane will redirect the query to the corresponding subsystem endpoint.

3.2.1.2 Authorization

After performing the whole authentication flow, clients will end up with two JWT tokens:

- **access_token:** Contains the subject id, together with the scope.
- **id_token:** Contains information about the user itself, including the Verifiable Credentials associated with the corresponding claims, based on the user profile.

Clients are expecting to provide those tokens in the header part when querying a secured endpoint. Figure 3.3 illustrates the authorization flow.

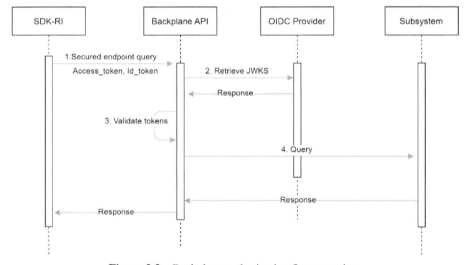

Figure 3.3   Backplane authorization flow overview.

1. **Secured endpoint query:** Clients are expected to include the access_token and id_token headers when requesting a Backplane authenticated endpoint.

2. **Retrieve JWKS**[4]**:** The OIDC uses token asynchronous validation; so the Backplane just needs to retrieve the JWKS, an array of public cryptographic keys, in order to validate each token in offline mode using EdDSA[5], a public-key cryptography signature algorithm.

3. **Validate tokens:** The Backplane internally validates the tokens' signature and verifies that the user has the required claims to access the endpoint.

4. **Query:** The query is redirected to the subsystem, together with the id_token header, containing a JWT token that describes the requester.

3.2.2 Subsystem implementation

While subsystems do not need to worry about authentication, they need to indicate in their OAS specification which of their endpoints are protected and which are not. To mark an endpoint as protected, it must include:

- **JWT security reference:** The endpoint specification must show that JWT is used as a means of authentication. This is done by adding de JWT schema to the security field, specifying if needed the claims required to access the endpoint.

```
"security": [
  {
    "jwt": ["consumer"]
  }
]
```

Then, clients must define the security schema as an ApiKey, expected to be presented in the header *id_token*:

- **JWT security schema:** Add the following security schema to the subsystem OpenApi specification (OAS):

```
"securitySchemes":{
"jwt":{
    "type": "apiKey",
    "in": "header",
    "name": "id_token"
  }
},
```

---

[4]JSON Web Key Sets (https://auth0.com/docs/secure/tokens/json-web-tokens/json-web-key-sets).

[5]https://www.rfc-editor.org/rfc/rfc8032

Note: There is no need to define the *access_token* explained before, as it is only being used by the Backplane itself; so, subsystems can ignore it.

With the above-stated OAS modifications, the service integrator engine will add the required authorization mechanism to each endpoint, automatically, during Backplane deployment pipeline, as described in Section 3.2.5.

3.2.3 Data flows

When a service is integrated into the Backplane, it means that its resources can be accessed through the Backplane itself. So, when a client application accesses to a resource into the Backplane, it will redirect the request to the final resource path, specified in the resource provider OAS file.

Thanks to this approach, the client is agnostic of the final location of the required service, being all handled by the Backplane.

The Backplane establishes a communication using JWT authentication between the Backplane and the service to ensure data protection. This communication can also be easily secured using certificates HTTPs/TLS.

3.2.4 Service Integration Manager

The service integration manager is one of the key components of the i3-MARKET Backplane. It ensures the easy integration of any subsystem service to the i3-MARKET Backplane, using OpenAPI specification as bridge.

The Manager is written in Dart[6] and is the one responsible for external service integration to the Backplane API; so it is capable of acting as a gateway for this new service. In Figure 3.4, there is an overview of how the service integration manager works, proceeding with the following steps:

1. **Generate resources:** Given a new service OpenAPI specification, it runs the Loopback CLI OpenAPI generator command[7], which generates the specified *controllers* and *data sources* that later will be integrated into the final Backplane API Docker image.
2. **Integrate + Build:** As the Loopback CLI just provides a set of skeletons, some modifications need to be performed to the previously generated sources, customizing them for our use case. Then, it can be integrated to the Backplane API base code, building the final Backplane Docker image, ready to be used for deployment.

---

[6]https://dart.dev/
[7]https://loopback.io/doc/en/lb4/OpenAPI-generator.html

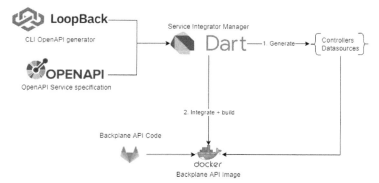

Figure 3.4 Service integrator process overview.

3.2.5 Automatic integration mechanism

In order to provide an easy onboarding experience, it is mandatory to build mechanisms to achieve easy and automated marketplaces and service integration. In order to achieve these goals, the consortium decided to use GitLab CI pipelines[8] together with Ansible playbooks[9], being GitLab responsible of artifact generation and Ansible of the deployment to i3-MARKET nodes.

3.2.6 Subsystem OAS repository

The integration process begins when an i3-MARKET maintainer validates a given subsystem OAS (OpenApi specification) and, hence, merges a pull request into the master branch adding or modifying a definition.

The lack of validation proofs hinders the i3-MARKET maintainer job, causing sometimes the approval of OAS files with errors or incompatibilities, which in the end break the Backplane. At this point, we found the need of implementing a CI/CD pipeline with a job responsible for validating the files, together with the correct integration within the Backplane base code, as described in Figure 3.5, performing the following steps in order:

1. **Validate the OAS file:** All the OAS files are collected and the API definition of each one is validated, using the npm swagger-cli[10] utility.

---

[8]https://docs.gitlab.com/ee/ci/pipelines/
[9]https://docs.ansible.com/ansible/latest/user_guide/playbooks_intro.html
[10]https://www.npmjs.com/package/swagger-cli

2. **Clone Backplane repository:** In this step, we are cloning the Backplane repository. This is a needed step in order to verify the OAS files are compatible with the integrator and the Backplane itself.

3. **Integrate OAS:** In this step, using the latest integrator engine available, we are integrating all the OAS files into the base Backplane code. In case some error or incompatibly is reported, the whole pipeline fails and notifies the i3-MARKET maintainer.

4. **Integration test:** This step starts a Backplane instance only accessible locally. Then, using a tool called schemathesis[11], we are testing all the endpoints of the Greeter subsystem[12], making sure none of them return an error 5XX. Note the tool is not testing all the subsystem endpoints, given the fact that we cannot assume the status of all of them. We found out that scanning a single known subsystem is enough to detect common failures.

5. **Release new version:** At this moment, we could say the OAS files are safe to be deployed; so, a new tag is being created and pushed into the Backplane repository. Triggering the Backplane automatic integration pipeline is explained in the next section.

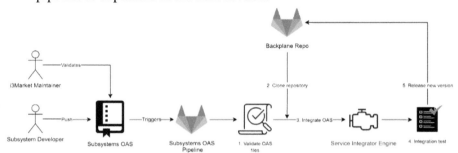

Figure 3.5   Subsystem OAS automatic integration mechanism overview.

3.2.7 Backplane repository

Validated updates on the subsystem OAS repository trigger the Backplane automatic integration mechanism, described in Figure 3.6, performing the following steps in order:

1. **Run the service integrator engine:** The engine artifact is collected from the corresponding code repository, and the code components that

---

[11] https://github.com/schemathesis/schemathesis

[12] Mockup of an OAS subsystem, created as an example for the rest of partners.

later will be integrated to the final Backplane artifact are generated. The functionality of the service integrator is fully explained in the previous section.

2. **Check vulnerabilities:** In this phase, a vulnerability check using Trivy[13] is performed, a vulnerability scanner developed by AquaSecurity[14]. This step scans NPM and OS libraries, marking the pipeline as failed in case any critical vulnerability is found.

3. **Integration test:** This step verifies the functionality of the fully integrated Backplane, as explained in the section before (subsystem OAS repository).

4. **Build image:** Using the code stored in the Backplane repository, together with the output of the service integrator, a new Docker image for production deployment is generated and uploaded to the project registry; so future deployment can easily be performed using Docker.

5. **Deploy:** The pipeline triggers the deployment Ansible playbooks, which deploy the Backplane API using the Docker image built previously, along with the i3-MARKET SDK Docker image.

6. **Update the developer portal:** In parallel to this process, because a new OAS has been uploaded to the project, the developer portal must be updated, triggering the documentation repository pipeline. It generates a new developer portal artifact and deploys it using GitLab Pages[15].

3.2.7.1 Remote images

All production-ready images can be found in the private and public repositories managed by the consortium (GitLab and Nexus). Currently, we are providing two different image flavours:

- **Major.minor.patch:** Base Backplane image, which includes the latest subsystem OAS available at the build instant.
- **Major.minor.patch-with-integrator:** Built from the base image, although it also includes the integrator binary under */integrator* path. This image provides a custom entry point that will check the existence of custom OAS files under */home/node/app/specs*. If affirmed, the integrator will integrate those specs into the base Backplane image before

---

[13]https://github.com/aquasecurity/trivy
[14]https://www.aquasec.com/
[15]https://docs.gitlab.com/ee/user/project/pages/

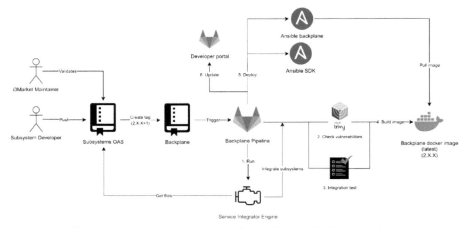

Figure 3.6   Backplane automatic integration mechanism overview.

running the Backplane; otherwise, the integration phase will be skipped, and the Backplane will be executed using the latest OAS definitions at the image compilation instant.

Both image flavours can be pulled using the described versioning format (*major.minor.patch*) or the *latest* tag to get the most recent version.

3.2.8 Final deployment

Final deployment phase, described in Figure 3.7, is orchestrated using a single Ansible playbook triggered by the GitLab CI pipeline described before. Actually, during this testing phase, four i3-MARKET nodes are being considered, each one performing the following tasks:

1. **Get config files:** Queries against i3-MARKET nexus repository are being executed in order to obtain the required configuration files for each node.
2. **Get Backplane Docker image:** The latest Backplane image is retrieved from the GitLab Docker image registry used in the artifact construction phase.
3. **Start Backplane container:** Now, the running container is replaced, launching a new one with the latest image, configuring the volumes and environment variables required.

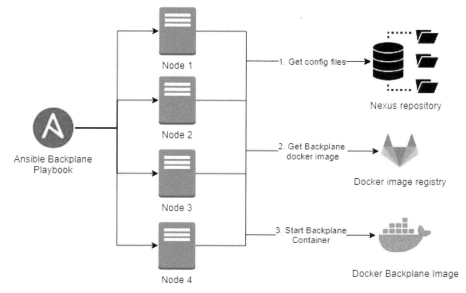

Figure 3.7   Ansible playbook run overview.

3.2.9 Multiple environments support

One of the limitations found in the current Backplane was the lack of support for multiple environment deployments. Specific OAS files had to be written for each environment, identical, except for the servers' annotation, that might differ based on the environment characteristics. Instead, we found out a way to support this requirement without having to duplicate OAS definitions.

Right now, we are using the Open API "servers" specification to indicate all servers providing the stated service, using custom tags to identify the ones to be used in each environment. For example:

```
{
    "servers": [
        {
          "url": "http://conflict-resolver-service:3000/",
          "x-tags": ["docker-compose"]
        },
        {
          "url": "http://node1.i3-MARKET.com:8888/",
          "x-tags": ["nodes"]
        },
        {
          "url": "http://node2.i3-MARKET.com:8888/",
          "x-tags": ["nodes"]
        }
    ],
}
```

In the previous definition, there are three different nodes providing the same service. Using the "x-tags," we can tag each server in order to choose at start-up time which set of servers has to use the Backplane to redirect the queries for each service.

The Backplane can filter and choose the most convenient server based on the *SERVER_FILTER_TAGS* environment variable definition, a comma separated list of tags to indicate the servers to use.

Figure 3.8 shows one server that can be used to redirect queries; hence, in case the previous selector gets multiple server options, a DNS resolution probe is executed for each hostname to choose the first available option. Given the heterogeneity of subsystems, the Backplane cannot assure availability of each server, as it lacks any liveness endpoint definition to test; furthermore, the Backplane is agnostic of the service functionality that it provides and its behaviour. Below, there is an example considering only the nodes tagged with "node," where node2 is being selected because node1 failed the DNS resolution.

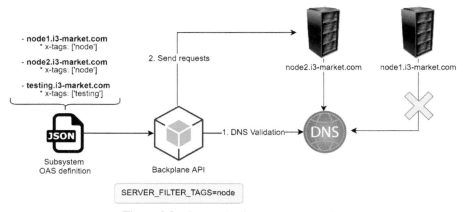

Figure 3.8   Server election process example.

We are aware that this approach is quite naïve, as host DNS availability does not prove there is a current API working in the server. However, it solves common issues of multiple environment deployments.

In order to improve the server election mechanism, we would need to enforce a liveness/readiness endpoint in marketplace definitions, which could also lead to including algorithms to failback to an alternative server in case the main one fails.

3.3 Interfaces

Backplane API for the i3-MARKET project:

3.3.1 Developers

`GET`/OpenIDConnectProvider/release2/developers/login

Obtain a valid initial_access_token for registering a new client

`POST`/OpenIDConnectProvider/release2/oidc/reg

Registering a new client

3.3.2 OIDC discovery

`GET`/OpenIDConnectProvider/release2/oidc/.well-known/openid-configuration

Get OpenID Provider configuration information

3.3.3 OIDC core

`GET`/OpenIDConnectProvider/release2/oidc/auth

Request authorization code

`GET`/OpenIDConnectProvider/release2/oidc/jwks

Get JSON Web Key Set

`POST`/OpenIDConnectProvider/release2/oidc/token

Request access token and id token with authorization code or refresh token

3.3.4 RegistryBlockchainController

`POST`/auditableAccounting/calculateMerkleRoot

`GET`/auditableAccounting/getCurrentRoot

`POST`/auditableAccounting/updateRegistries

3.3.5 RegistryController

`GET` `/auditableAccounting/registries/count`

`PUT` `/auditableAccounting/registries/{id}`

`PATCH` `/auditableAccounting/registries/{id}`

`GET` `/auditableAccounting/registries/{id}`

`DELETE` `/auditableAccounting/registries/{id}`

`POST` `/auditableAccounting/registries`

`PATCH` `/auditableAccounting/registries`

`GET` `/auditableAccounting/registries`

3.3.6 AuthController

`GET` `/auth/openid/callback`

`GET` `/auth/openid/login`

`GET` `/auth/whoAmI`

3.3.7 Conflict-resolver service

`POST` `/conflictResolverService/dispute`

Initiates a dispute claiming that a cipherblock cannot be decrypted and thus that the data exchange is invalid

`POST` `/conflictResolverService/verification`

Verification request of completeness of non-repudiation protocol regarding a data exchange

3.3.8 FarewellController

`POST` `/greeter/farewell/body`

`GET` `/greeter/farewell/headerParams`

`GET` `/greeter/farewell/pathParams/{name}/{age}`

`GET` `/greeter/farewell/queryParams`

3.3.9 HelloController

`GET`/greeter/hello/authenticated

`GET`/greeter/hello/consumer

`GET`/greeter/hello/provider

`GET`/greeter/hello/unauthenticated/{name}

3.3.10 OpenApiController

`GET`/notification-manager-oas/api/v1/health

Version

`GET`/notification-manager-oas/api/v1/version

Version

3.3.11 Notifications

`POST`/notification-manager-oas/api/v1/notification/service

Notification service

`GET`/notification-manager-oas/api/v1/notification/unread

Get unread notifications

`GET`/notification-manager-oas/api/v1/notification/user/{user id}/unread

Get unread notifications by id

`GET`/notification-manager-oas/api/v1/notification/user/{user id}

Get notification by Userid

`PATCH`/notification-manager-oas/api/v1/notification/{notification id}/read

Modify notification

`PATCH`/notification-manager-oas/api/v1/notification/{notification id}/unread

Modify notification

`GET`/notification-manager-oas/api/v1/notification/{notification id}

Get notification

`DELETE`/notification-manager-oas/api/v1/notification/{notification id}

Delete notification

`POST`/notification-manager-oas/api/v1/notification

Notification user

`GET`/notification-manager-oas/api/v1/notification

Get notifications

3.3.12 Queues

`PATCH` `/notification-manager-oas/api/v1/services/{service id}/queues/{queue id}/activate`

Switch status queue

`PATCH` `/notification-manager-oas/api/v1/services/{service id}/queues/{queue id}/deactivate`

Switch status queue

`GET` `/notification-manager-oas/api/v1/services/{service id}/queues/{queue id}`

Get queues by id

`DELETE` `/notification-manager-oas/api/v1/services/{service id}/queues/{queue id}`

Delete queue

`POST` `/notification-manager-oas/api/v1/services/{service id}/queues`

Post queues

`GET` `/notification-manager-oas/api/v1/services/{service id}/queues`

Get queues

`GET` `/notification-manager-oas/api/v1/services/{service id}`

Get services by id

`DELETE` `/notification-manager-oas/api/v1/services/{service id}`

Delete service

`POST` `/notification-manager-oas/api/v1/services`

Create service

`GET` `/notification-manager-oas/api/v1/services`

Get services

3.3.13 Subscriptions

`GET` `/notification-manager-oas/api/v1/users/subscriptions/{category}`

Returns a Json containing a list of users subscribed to that category

`GET` `/notification-manager-oas/api/v1/users/subscriptions`

Get all user subscriptions

`PATCH` `/notification-manager-oas/api/v1/users/{user id}/subscriptions/{subscription id}/activate`

Activate or deactivate user subscription

`PATCH` `/notification-manager-oas/api/v1/users/{user id}/subscriptions/{subscription id}/deactivate`

Activate or deactivate user subscription

`GET` `/notification-manager-oas/api/v1/users/{user id}/subscriptions/{subscription id}`

Get user subscription by user_id and subscription_id

`DELETE`/notification-manager-oas/api/v1/users/{user id}/subscriptions/{subscription id}

Delete subscription by user_id and subscription_id

`POST`/notification-manager-oas/api/v1/users/{user id}/subscriptions

Create subscription to category

`GET`/notification-manager-oas/api/v1/users/{user id}/subscriptions

Get Subscriptions by Userid

3.3.14 PingController

`GET`/ping

`GET`/pingConsumer

`GET`/pingProvider

`GET`/pingUser

3.3.15 Cost-controller

`GET`/pricingManager/fee/getfee

Get I3M fee

`PUT`/pricingManager/fee/setfee

Set I3M fee

3.3.16 Price-controller

`GET`/pricingManager/price/checkformulaconfiguration

Check formula and parameter consistency

`GET`/pricingManager/price/getformulajsonconfiguration

Get configuration using Json format

`GET`/pricingManager/price/getprice

Get the price of data

`PUT`/pricingManager/price/setformulaconstant

Set formula constant

`PUT`/pricingManager/price/setformulajsonconfiguration

Set configuration using Json format

`PUT`/pricingManager/price/setformulaparameter

Set formula parameter

`PUT`/pricingManager/price/setformulawithdefaultconfiguration

Set formula with default values for constants and parameters

3.3.17 RatingService

`GET`/rating/api/agreements/{id}/isRated

Check if an agreement is rated

`GET`/rating/api/agreements/{id}/rating

Get the rating object of a specified agreement

`GET`/rating/api/consumers/{pk}/agreements

Get the terminated agreements of the consumer

`GET`/rating/api/consumers/{did}/ratings

Get the ratings of the consumer

`GET`/rating/api/providers/{pk}/agreements

Get the terminated agreements of the provider

`GET`/rating/api/providers/{did}/ratings

Get the ratings of the provider

`GET`/rating/api/providers/{did}/totalRating

Get the average rating of the provider

`GET`/rating/api/questions

Get all the questions

`POST`/rating/api/ratings/{id}/respond

Respond to a rating object

`PUT`/rating/api/ratings/{id}

Edit an existing Rating

`GET`/rating/api/ratings/{id}

Get a single rating.

`DELETE`/rating/api/ratings/{id}

Delete a single rating.

`POST`/rating/api/ratings

Create a new rating

`GET`/rating/api/ratings

Get all the ratings

3.3.18 Agreement

`GET`/sc-manager-oas/check active agreements

Check active agreements

`POST`/sc-manager-oas/check agreements by consumer

Check agreements by consumer

`GET`/sc-manager-oas/check agreements by data offering/{offering id}

Check agreements by data offering

`POST`/sc-manager-oas/check agreements by provider

Check agreements by provider

`POST`/sc-manager-
oas/create agreement raw transaction/{sender address}

Create agreement

`POST`/sc-manager-oas/deploy signed transaction

Deploy signed transaction

`PUT`/sc-manager-oas/enforce penalty

Enforce penalty

`POST`/sc-manager-oas/evaluate signed resolution

Verify a signed resolution

`GET`/sc-manager-oas/get agreement/{agreement id}

Get agreement

`GET`/sc-manager-oas/get pricing model/{agreement id}

Get agreement's pricing model

`GET`/sc-manager-oas/get state/{agreement id}

Get the state of the agreement

`POST`/sc-manager-oas/propose penalty

Choose penalty

`GET`/sc-manager-oas/retrieve agreements/{consumer public key}

Retrieve the active agreements, which start date is reached, based on consumer public key

`GET`/sc-manager-oas/template/{offering id}

Request template with static and dynamic parameters

`PUT`/sc-manager-oas/terminate

Terminate agreement

3.3.19 Explicit user consent

`GET`/sc-manager-oas/check consent status/{dataOfferingId}

Check consent status

`POST`/sc-manager-oas/deploy consent signed transaction

Deploy consent signed transaction

`POST`/sc-manager-oas/give consent

Give consent

`PUT`/sc-manager-oas/revoke consent

Revoke consent

3.3.20 Registration-offering

`GET`/semantic-
engine/api/registration/ActiveOfferingByCategory/{category}

Get a registered active data offerings by category

`GET`/semantic-
engine/api/registration/ActiveOfferingByProvider/{id}/providerId

Get a registered active data offering by provider

`GET`/semantic-engine/api/registration/categories-list

Get a list of all categories

`GET`/semantic-engine/api/registration/contract-
parameter/{offeringId}/offeringId

Get contract parameters by offering id

`POST`/semantic-engine/api/registration/data-offering

Register a data offering

`DELETE`/semantic-engine/api/registration/delete-offering/{id}

Delete a data offering

`GET`/semantic-engine/api/registration/federated-
activeOffering/{id}/providerId

Get a registered active data offering by provider

`GET`/semantic-engine/api/registration/federated-
activeOffering/{category}

Get a registered active federated data offering by category

`GET`/semantic-engine/api/registration/federated-contract-
parameter/{id}/offeringId

Get contract parameters by offering id in federated search

`GET`/semantic-engine/api/registration/federated-
offering/getActiveOfferingByText/{text}/text

Get a registered data offering by text/keyword

`GET`/semantic-engine/api/registration/federated-
offering/textSearch/text/{text}

Get a registered data offering by text/keyword in federated search

`GET`/semantic-engine/api/registration/federated-
offering/{id}/offeringId

Get a registered data offering by offering id

`GET`/semantic-engine/api/registration/federated-offering/{category}

Get a registered data offering by category

`GET`/semantic-engine/api/registration/federated-offerings-list/on-
Active

Get a list of offerings for active in federated search

`GET`/semantic-engine/api/registration/federated-offerings-list/on-
SharedNetwork

Get a list of offerings for shared status in federated search

`GET`/semantic-engine/api/registration/federated-offerings-list

Get a list of offerings

`GET`/semantic-engine/api/registration/federated-providers-list

Get a list of providers

`GET`**/semantic-engine/api/registration/getActiveOfferingByText/{text}/text**

Get a registered data offering by text/keyword

`GET`**/semantic-engine/api/registration/getOfferingByActiveAndShareDataWithThirdParty/{active}/{shareDataWithThirdParty}**

Get a registered data offering by active and sharedWithThirdParty status

`GET`**/semantic-engine/api/registration/getOfferingBySharedAndTransferableAndFreePrice/{shared}/{transfer}/{freePrice}**

Get a registered data offering by shared and transferable and FreePrice status

`GET`**/semantic-engine/api/registration/offering/ByTitleAndPricingModelName/{dataOfferingTitle}/{pricingModelName}**

Get a registered data offering by title and pricing model name

`GET`**/semantic-engine/api/registration/offering/offering-template**

Download offering template

`GET`**/semantic-engine/api/registration/offering/provider/{providerId}**

Get data provider by providerId

`GET`**/semantic-engine/api/registration/offering/{id}/offeringId**

Get a registered data offering by offering id

`GET`**/semantic-engine/api/registration/offering/{id}/providerId**

Get a registered data offering by provider id

`GET`**/semantic-engine/api/registration/offering/{category}**

Get a registered data offering by category

`GET`**/semantic-engine/api/registration/offerings**

Get total offering and its list

`GET`**/semantic-engine/api/registration/offerings-list/on-SharedNetwork**

Get a list of offerings for shared status

`GET`**/semantic-engine/api/registration/offerings-list/on-active**

Get a list of offerings for active

`GET`**/semantic-engine/api/registration/offerings-list**

Get a list of offerings

`DELETE`**/semantic-engine/api/registration/provider/{providerId}/delete**

Delete a data provider by providerId

`GET`**/semantic-engine/api/registration/providers/{category}/category**

Get a list of providers by category

`GET`**/semantic-engine/api/registration/providers-list**

Get a list of providers

`GET`/semantic-engine/api/registration/textSearch/text/{text}

Get a registered data offering by text/keyword

`PUT`/semantic-engine/api/registration/update-offering

Update already registered offering info

`POST`/semantic-engine/api/registration

Register provider info

3.3.21 TokenizerController

`POST`/tokenization/api/v1/operations/clearing

Retrieve the transaction object to start the marketplace clearing operation

`POST`/tokenization/api/v1/operations/exchange-in

Retrieve the transaction object to perform an exchangeIn.

`POST`/tokenization/api/v1/operations/exchange-out

Retrieve the transaction object to perform an exchangeOut

`POST`/tokenization/api/v1/operations/fee-payment

Generate the fee payment transaction object

`POST`/tokenization/api/v1/operations/set-paid

Generate the payment transaction object

`GET`/tokenization/api/v1/operations

Get list of operations

`GET`/tokenization/api/v1/treasury/balances/{address}

Get the balance for a specific account

`POST`/tokenization/api/v1/treasury/community-wallet

Alter the community wallet address and the related community fee

`GET`/tokenization/api/v1/treasury/marketplaces/{address}

Get the index of a registered marketplace

`POST`/tokenization/api/v1/treasury/marketplaces

Register a marketplace

`GET`/tokenization/api/v1/treasury/token-transfers/{transferId}

Get the token transfer given a TransferId

`POST`/tokenization/api/v1/treasury/transactions/deploy-signed-transaction

Deploy a signed transaction

`GET`/tokenization/api/v1/treasury/transactions/{transactionHash}

Get the receipt of a transaction given a TransactionHash

3.3.22 Credential

`GET` `/verifiableCredentials/release2/vc/credential/issue/{credential}/callbackUrl/{callbackUrl}`

Create a new credential with Veramo framework and store it in the wallet (full flow)

`GET` `/verifiableCredentials/release2/vc/credential/issue/{did}/{credential}`

Generate a new credential with Veramo framework for a specific DID

`POST` `/verifiableCredentials/release2/vc/credential/revoke`

Revoke a credential by JWT

`POST` `/verifiableCredentials/release2/vc/credential/verify`

Verify a credential by JWT

`GET` `/verifiableCredentials/release2/vc/credential`

Get the credential list

3.3.23 Issuer

`GET` `/verifiableCredentials/release2/vc/issuer/subscribe`

Subscribe this issuer in the i3-MARKET trusted issuers list

`GET` `/verifiableCredentials/release2/vc/issuer/unsubscribe`

Unsubscribe this issuer from the i3-MARKET trusted issuers list

`GET` `/verifiableCredentials/release2/vc/issuer/verify`

Verify the subscription status of the issuer

4

Deployment Guides

This section aims to explain how to deploy software within the i3-MARKET Backplane instances.

4.1 Artifact Deployment Guides

The target audience are the i3-MARKET project developers who are participating in the development and deployment of the i3-MARKET Backplane.

The i3-MARKET operative considers four possible deployment scenarios, categorized into manual and automatized deployments. These scenarios are the following:

- Manual deployment scenario one (MDS1)
- Automatized deployment scenario with Ansible (ADS1)
- Automatized deployment scenario with Ansible and GitHub CI/CD (ADS2)
- Automatized deployment scenario with Docker Compose (ADS3)

Considering an i3-MARKET user role perspective, the main roles involved in the different deployment scenarios are:

- i3M root instance admin
- i3M SW developer
- i3M third-party SW admin
- i3M pilot instance admin

Table 4.1 provides the mapping between the i3-MARKET user roles and the previously listed deployment scenarios.

The following subsections describe in detail each identified deployment scenario.

Table 4.1   Deployment scenarios and i3M user roles mapping.

Deployment scenario/user role	i3M root instance admin	i3M SW developer	i3M third-party SW admin	i3M pilot instance admin
MDS1	✗	✓	✓	✓
ADS1	✓	✗	✓	✓
ADS2	✗	✓	✗	✓
ADS3	✓	✓	✗	✓

4.2 MDS1: Manual Deployment

The manual deployment scenario one (MDS1) is based on accessing the physical resources by establishing an SSH connection. Once the physical resource is accessed, the user proceeds with the SW deployment manually. An overview of MDS1 is provided in Figure 4.1. The actors involved in these scenarios are i3M SW developer and i3M third-party SW admin; see Figure 4.1.

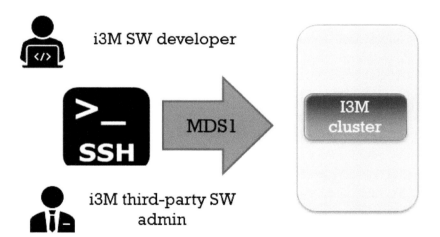

Figure 4.1   MDS1.

4.3 ADS1: Automatized Deployment with Ansible Scenario One

Automated deployment scenario one (ADS1) is based on the provision of a set of Ansible playbooks containing deployment recipes. Playbooks are one of the core features of Ansible and tell Ansible what to execute. They are like a to-do list for Ansible that contains a list of tasks. Playbooks contain the steps that the user wants to execute on a concrete physical resource, and they are run sequentially. From an operative point of view, actors involved in this scenario must cover the following deployment workflow:

1) Create an Ansible template (playbook) with concrete deployment instructions using the physical resources specified in Section 4.3.
2) Start an Ansible job by instantiating the playbook template provided in step 1.

An overview of ADS1 is provided in Figure 4.2. The actors involved in this scenario are i3M IT admin and i3M third-party SW admin.

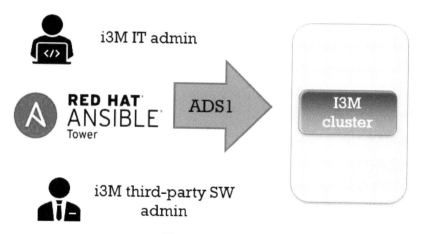

Figure 4.2 ADS1.

Finally, Figure 4.3 contains a playbook example showing the main structure in terms of tags to be included in i3-MARKET playbooks, which are: name, hosts, vars, and tasks.

```
---
name: install and configure DB
hosts: testServer
become: yes

vars:
    oracle_db_port_value : 1521

tasks:
-name: Install the Oracle DB
    yum: <code to install the DB>

-name: Ensure the installed service is enabled and running
service:
    name: <your service name>
```

Figure 4.3   Ansible playbook example.

4.4 ADS2: Automated Deployment with Ansible and CI/CD GitHub Pipelines Two

Automatized deployment scenario two (ADS2) is based on the provision of CI/CD pipelines with Ansible and GitHub. The only actor involved in this scenario is i3-MARKET SW developer. The goal to reach in current deployment scenario should be aligned with i3-MARKET DevOps strategy and based on the provision of an Ansible Tower CI/CD architecture.

An overview of ADS2 is provided in Figure 4.4. The only actor involved in this scenario is i3M SW developer.

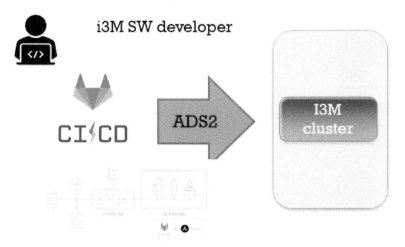

Figure 4.4   ADS2.

The goal to reach in current deployment scenario should be aligned with i3-MARKET DevOps strategy [3] and based on the provision of an Ansible Tower CI/CD architecture.

Considering the approach presented in [4], Figure 4.5 illustrates what we should build to support CI/CD in i3-MARKET using Ansible and GitHub.

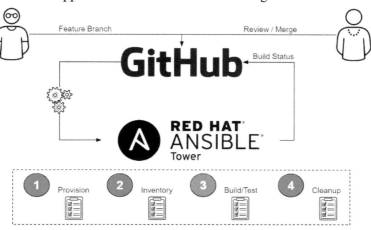

Figure 4.5 i3-MARKET CI/CD with Ansible and GitHub.

As is well known, the main purpose of CI is of course to protect the master branch so that it always compiles. The only way to do this is to check the code in another branch (like a function branch), test that code, review the code, and only merge it with the master once all tests pass. The architecture above achieves exactly that and does so with a very simplified approach that leverages Ansible Tower as our CI engine. For the CD part, only a few additional workflows would be needed to implement artifacts generated by the CI process in dev -> test -> production. Using this architecture, one could use the GitHub versions to store artifacts. GitHub has the ability to trigger a webhook when the latest version is updated, which in turn could trigger an Ansible Tower CD workflow.

4.5 ADS3: Automated Deployment with Docker Compose

The last way of automatizing the deployments on i3-MARKET is by means of Docker Compose[1]. After the last release of the deployment strategy adopted by i3-MARKET of having *N* decentralized i3-MARKET instances + 1 master

---

[1] https://docs.docker.com/compose/

i3-MARKET instance for centralizing some services, a deployment for supporting the installation of an i3-MARKET instance (a decentralized node) has been created based on Docker Compose. This Docker Compose is used for deploying and managing multiple Docker containers, each of them containing different core and decentralized services developed by i3-MARKET.

This mechanism will allow any marketplace to deploy an i3-MARKET "pilot environment" in order to be part and interact with the i3-MARKET ecosystem. Therefore, ADS3 becomes the most useful deployment strategy for supporting i3-MARKET pilots in the deployment of those i3-MARKET services, which need to be decentralized and installed in the pilot premises. These services are (see more details in Table 2.6): "backplane" (Backplane API component), "tokenizer" + "pricing-manager" (Monetization component), "sdk-ref-impl" (SDK-RI component), "web-ri" + "mongo_web-ri" (Web-RI), "oidc-provider-app" + "oidc-provider-db" (Service-centric authentication component), "vc-service" (User-centric authentication component), semantic-engine + semantic-engine-db (Semantic engine component), data_access (Data access component), auditable-accounting (Auditable accounting component), besu (Blockchain network pilot node + RocksDB instance), cockroachdb-node (Distributed storage component), conflict-resolver-service (Conflict resolution component), rating (Rating component), and "keycloak" (Security server component).

In terms of the Docker Compose file definition, a set of ".env.*component*" files has been created for storing config information relative to the deployment of each of the services contained in the Docker Compose file. For a first idea of the compose file, see below in Table 4.2 the header as reference of it.

Table 4.2   i3m-pilots-docker-compose.yml.

```
version: '3'
services:
  backplane:
    container_name: backplane
    image: "XX.XX.XX.XX:XXXX/backplane:${BACKPLANE_VERSION}"
    restart: unless-stopped
    ports:
      - 3000:3000
    env_file: .env.backplane
    networks:
      - i3m-net
    healthcheck:
      test: "exit 0"
  tokenizer:
```

```
    image: registry.gitlab.com/i3-market/code/wp3/t3.3/nodejs-tokenization-treasury-api:${TOKENIZER_VERSION}
    container_name: tokenizer
    ports:
      - 3001:3001
    env_file: .env.tokenizer
    restart: unless-stopped
    networks:
      - i3m-net
    depends_on:
      besu:
        condition: service_healthy
      postgres:
        condition: service_healthy
  sdk-ri:
    image: registry.gitlab.com/i3-market/code/sdk/i3m-sdk-reference-implementation/sdk-ri:${SDKRI_VERSION}
    container_name: sdk-ref-impl
    restart: unless-stopped
    env_file: .env.sdk-ri
    ports:
      - 8181:8080
    networks:
      - i3m-net
    depends_on:
      backplane:
        condition: service_healthy
    command: java -jar /usr/local/jetty/start.jar
    healthcheck:
      test: "exit 0"
  web-ri:
    image: registry.gitlab.com/i3-market/code/web-ri/web-ri:${WEB_RI_VERSION}
    container_name: web-ri
    ports:
      - 5300:3000
    env_file: .env.web-ri
    restart: unless-stopped
    networks:
      - i3m-net
    depends_on:
      - mongo_web-ri
    healthcheck:
      test: "exit 0"
  mongo_web-ri:
    image: mongo:${MONGO_WEBRI_VERSION}
    container_name: mongo_web-ri
    ports:
```

```
 - 27017:27017
restart: unless-stopped
env_file: .env.web-ri
networks:
 - i3m-net
command: --quiet --setParameter logLevel=0
```

Besides installing the decentralized services by means of the Docker Compose file, the administrator of the pilot infrastructure must install a wallet.

4.6 Tagging Releases Strategy

i3-MARKET has evolved into a complex system where a large number of pieces must interact together for a comprehensive and integrated performance. Therefore, the different versions released by each single component/microservice should be managed and controlled to avoid incompatibilities in the deployments.

A strategy based on tagging and a compatibility matrix has been defined to deal with the release's compatibility.

Thus, every version released by a component is formatted as MAJOR.MINOR.PATCH tag, and each part changes according to the following rules.

We increment:

- MAJOR when breaking backward compatibility;
- MINOR when adding a new feature which does not break compatibility;
- PATCH when fixing a bug without breaking compatibility.

On the other hand, a matrix including the "microservice name", "microservice version", and a vector of dependencies with other components (and its compatible version) has been defined.

4.7 Deployment Process

At the deployment time, each artifact/service must include in the associated git project a requirements.txt file providing values in the "USES" columns; for example, see the requirement.txt for semantic engine in Figure 4.6.

- WALLET_APP = ""
- CLOUD _WALLET = ""
- VC = ""
- OIDC = ""
- DATA_ACCESS = ""
- NM = ""
- TOKENIZER = ""
- DS = ""
- AUDITABLE_ACCOUNTING = ""
- SCM = ""
- BESU = ""
- SEMANTIC_ENGINE = ""
- BACKPLANE_API = "V2.1.0 "
- SDK-RI = "V2.1.1 "
- WEB-RI = "V2.1.1"

Figure 4.6   Requirement.txt for semantic engine repository.

4.7.1 Docker Compose

Docker Compose is a tool for defining and running multi-container Docker applications. It allows you to define the services and their dependencies in a YAML file and run them with a single command. Docker Compose is especially useful for complex applications that require multiple containers, such as web applications that use a database and a web server.

The Docker Compose file defines the services, networks, and volumes for the application. Each service is defined with its own Docker image, command, environment variables, ports, and volumes. Dependencies between services can be specified using network connections, and shared volumes can be defined to allow data to be shared between containers.

Docker Compose can be used to orchestrate the deployment of containers in a local development environment or in a production environment. It can be used with Docker Swarm to deploy multi-node applications, and it can be integrated with other tools such as Jenkins or GitLab CI/CD for continuous integration and continuous deployment.

Using Docker Compose can provide many benefits for your Docker-based applications, including the following.

1) **Simplified deployment:** Docker Compose makes it easy to deploy multi-container applications with a single command.

2) **Improved scalability:** By defining services and their dependencies, Docker Compose allows you to scale individual components of your application as needed.

3) **Consistent environments:** Docker Compose ensures that all services in your application run in a consistent environment, regardless of the host system.

4) **Easy testing:** Docker Compose makes it easy to spin up test environments with the same configuration as your production environment.

5) **Better collaboration:** By defining the application configuration in a YAML file, Docker Compose makes it easy to share and collaborate on configurations with other team members.

Docker Compose is a powerful tool for defining and deploying multi-container Docker applications. It simplifies the deployment process and allows you to scale your applications with ease, while also ensuring consistency across environments and enabling collaboration between team members.

4.7.2 Technical Requirements

The technical requirements for using Docker Compose include:

1) **Docker Engine:** Docker Compose requires Docker Engine to be installed and running on the host system. Docker Engine is a container runtime that allows you to build, run, and manage Docker containers.

2) **YAML file:** Docker Compose uses a YAML file to define the services, networks, and volumes for the application. The YAML file should be named docker-compose.yml and should be located in the root directory of the application.

3) **Docker images:** Docker Compose uses Docker images to create containers for each service in the application. Docker images can be obtained from Docker Hub, a public registry of Docker images, or from a private registry.

4) **Network connections:** Services in the application may need to communicate with each other over the network. Docker Compose uses Docker networks to create isolated network environments for each application.

5) **Volumes:** Docker Compose allows you to define volumes to share data between containers and persist data beyond the life of a container. Volumes can be defined as local host directories or as named volumes.

6) **Environment variables:** Docker Compose allows you to define environment variables for each service in the application. Environment variables can be used to configure the behaviour of the container at runtime.

7) **Compose CLI:** Docker Compose can be run from the command line using the Compose CLI. The Compose CLI allows you to start, stop, and manage Docker Compose applications.

Docker Compose requires a basic understanding of Docker and containerization concepts, as well as familiarity with YAML syntax. It is recommended to have a solid understanding of Docker Engine before using Docker Compose, as it relies heavily on Docker Engine functionality.

4.7.3 Specification and configurations

The specification and configurations of Docker Compose are defined in a YAML file named "docker-compose.yml". This file consists of several sections that define the services, networks, and volumes for the application.

1) **Version:** The version section specifies the version of the Compose file format to use. The latest version is version 3.9, but earlier versions may be used depending on the Docker Engine version being used.

2) **Services:** The services section defines the individual services that make up the application. Each service is defined as a separate block, with its own image, environment variables, ports, volumes, and other configuration options.

3) **Networks:** The networks section defines the networks that the services use to communicate with each other. By default, Docker Compose creates a network for the application, but additional networks can be defined as needed.

4) **Volumes:** The volumes section defines the volumes that are used by the services to store persistent data. Volumes can be defined as named volumes or as host directories.

5) **Environment variables:** The environment section defines environment variables that are passed to the services. Environment variables can be used to configure the behaviour of the container at runtime.

6) **Deploy:** The deploy section specifies additional deployment options for the services, such as the number of replicas, placement constraints, and resource limits.

7) **External services:** The external_services section is used to define services that are provided by external sources, such as a load balancer or a database that is not part of the Docker Compose application.

These sections can be further configured with various options, such as image pull policies, container restart policies, logging options, and more.

4.7.4 Deployment

This Docker Compose is used for deploying and managing multiple docker containers, each of them containing different core and decentralized services developed by i3-MARKET. Therefore, ADS3 becomes the most useful deployment strategy for supporting i3-MARKET pilots in the deployment of those i3-MARKET services, which need to be decentralized and installed in the pilot premises. It is a practical guide that makes use of the automated deployment based on Docker Compose (ADS3).

The required steps are:

1) **Clone i3-MARKET deployment repository:**

Execute the following command:

```
git clone https://i3m-hackathon-user:userX@github.com/i3-Market-V2-Public-Repository/Support---Deployment-Tools.git
```

2) **Login into i3-MARKET Nexus and GitLab:**

Execute the following two commands:

```
docker login -u i3m-hackathon -p i3m-hackathon X.X.X.X:XXXX


docker login -u i3m-hackathon-user -p userX registry.gitlab.com
```

3) **Execute docker compose:**

Go to your cloned_dir/docker-compose/i3m-instance and execute the following command:

```
docker-compose --env-file .env -f .\i3m-pilots-docker-compose.yml up
```

To stop services:

```
docker-compose --env-file .env -f .\i3m-pilots-docker-compose.yml down
```

To verify that all services are up and running:

If you have Docker Desktop installed, you can view all running containers under the "i3m-instance" as shown in the following image:

5

Operative Specification

An operational specification provides a comprehensive overview of how the software is expected to function in various operating conditions. It serves as a road map for software development and testing and ensures that the final product meets the user's requirements and expectations.

5.1 Libraries

The list of the different libraries used to integrate into the i3-MARKET framework is shown below.

Auditable accounting library:

○ The auditable accounting component is a service that includes an API to automate the process of logging and auditing interactions between components and record the registries in the blockchain. The API of the auditable accounting is accessed through the Backplane API gateway. Additionally, the auditable accounting component can be accessed directly from any internal component of the platform.
○ License: MIT.
○ Source code: https://gitlab.com/i3-market-v3-public-repository/sp3-sc gbssw-aa-auditableaccounting.
○ Prerequisites: Node.js, Docker, and Docker Compose.

Wallet client library:

○ This package defines how to interact with wallets by means of a typescript interface. Furthermore, it provides a default implementation called BaseWallet. It uses an interface called KeyWallet to delegate the complexity of key management to other packages like SW Wallet. Both interfaces are listed below.
○ License: Apache License 2.0.

○ Source code: https://gitlab.com/i3-market-v3-public-repository/sp3-sc gbssw-i3mwalletmonorepo.
○ Prerequisites: Node.js.

5.2 i3-MARKET APIs

The update compared to R1 in terms of common services is the following:

i) Notification manager common services: The functionalities related with notification services and queues were the scope of R2 and R3 and are listed in Figure 5.1.

Figure 5.1 Services and queues common services.

ii) Alerts common services: The functionalities related with alerts were the scope of R2 and R3 and are listed in Figures 5.2, 5.3, and 5.4.

Figure 5.2 Alerts common services.

iii) Conflict resolution common services:
The functionalities related with contradictory conditions enabled by two methods as shown in Figure 5.3

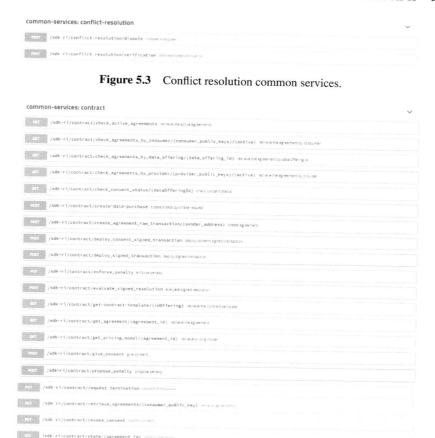

common-services: conflict-resolution

POST /sdk-ri/conflict-resolution/dispute *initiates a dispute*

POST /sdk-ri/conflict-resolution/verification *data exchange verification*

Figure 5.3 Conflict resolution common services.

common-services: contract

Figure 5.4 Contracts common services.

iv) Contracts common services: The functionalities related with smart contracts management were the scope of R2 and R3 and are listed in Figure 5.5.

v) Credential common services: The functionalities related with authentication, identities, and credentials were the scope of R2 and R3 and are listed in 5.5.

vi) Exchange common services: The functionalities related with data exchange were the scope of R2 and R3 and are listed in Figure 5.6.

Figure 5.5   Contracts common services.

Figure 5.6   Exchange common services.

vii) Notification common services: The functionalities related with notifications were the scope of R2 and R3 and are listed in Figure 5.7.

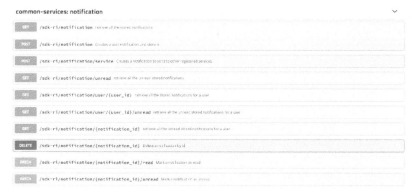

Figure 5.7   Notification common services.

viii) Offering management common services: The functionalities related with
data offering management were the scope of R2 and R3 and are listed in
Figure 5.8.

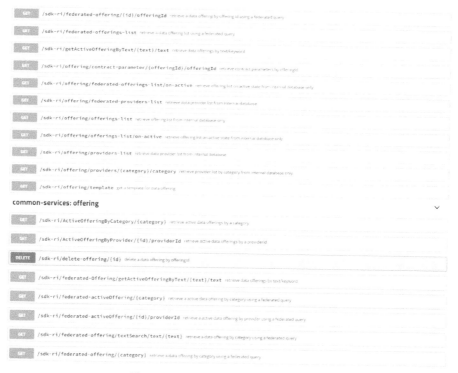

Figure 5.8 Offering common services.

ix) Pricing managing common services: The functionalities related with pricing managing were the scope of R2 and R3 and are listed in Figure 5.9.

Figure 5.9   Pricing common services.

x) Token managing common services: The functionalities related with token management were the scope of R2 and R3 and are listed in Figure 5.10.

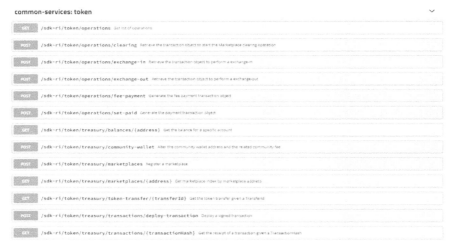

Figure 5.10   Tokens common services.

5.3 SDKs

The layered SDK approach defined in the mechanism allows to adapt and extend existing data marketplaces to interface with the i3-MARKET Backplane.

Specifically, the layers that are part of the proposed solution for the SDK are the following:

- **SDK-core:** This layer aims to simplify the i3-MARKET SDK building process by generating client stubs for any i3-MARKET backend endpoint/API, defined with the OpenAPI (formerly known as Swagger) specification. In this way, therefore, the development team can better focus on the implementation and adoption of these backend endpoints or APIs.
- **SDK reference implementation (SDK-RI):** This layer aims to identify and provide a set of common services to be implemented for consuming available Backplane functionalities.
- **SDK-execution patterns (SDK-EP):** It is including the atomic functions that make use of Backplane API (via SDK) adding some business logic.
- **SDK Web-RI:** It is supporting the frontend or GUI integrating the common services provided by the SDK-RI and that can be reused and customized as part of the pilot specification and implementation defined in the context of WP5.

5.4 User Interfaces

To contextualize the i3-MARKET frontend or SDK Web-RI, it is important to introduce the SDK global approach and is shown in Figure 5.11. SDK Web-RI would be the top layer on the layered approach defined as part of the SDK solution for i3-MARKET.

i3-MARKET Web-RI provides a graphical user interface component, designed to use the reference implementation (SDK-RI) through a user interface to validate i3-MARKET functionalities from the user's point of view. It will be provided as an open-source component for the i3-MARKET implementation and for future pilots.

Web-RI can be used also by other market players to easily integrate with i3-MARKET and even set up a marketplace. Web-RI implements the following basic workflows:

- Register new data offerings and delete data offerings
- Search for offerings
- Create and sign smart contracts
- Purchase data
- Pay for data

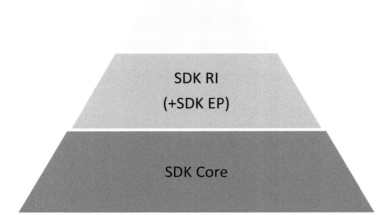

Figure 5.11   Implementation pyramid.

- Transfer data
- Rate data providers

  This section aims to explain how an end-user can operate within the i3-MARKET user interface.

5.5 Install i3M Wallet

Go to repo URL (https://github.com/i3-Market-V3-Public-Repository/SP3-SCGBSSW-I3mWalletMonorepo/releases) and download the v2.5.6 version suitable for your operating system and do the following actions for:

- Windows operating system:
    - Download and execute wallet-desktop-v2.5.6-x64.exe.
    - The application is a standalone RAR file. Extract it and execute the i3M Wallet.exe file.
- MacOS operating system:
    - Open the dmg file and install the wallet desktop application.

- Linux operating system:
  - ○ For Debian-based systems, you can use the deb package:
- \# change x.x.x for the version.
- sudo dpkg-i wallet-desktop-x.x.x-amd64.deb.

5.6 Create a Wallet and a Consumer and/or Provider Identity in the Wallet

The first time a user initiates the application, a dialog asking for a password appears (see following pictures for more details). The user will have to introduce this password each time the application starts – see Figure 5.12.

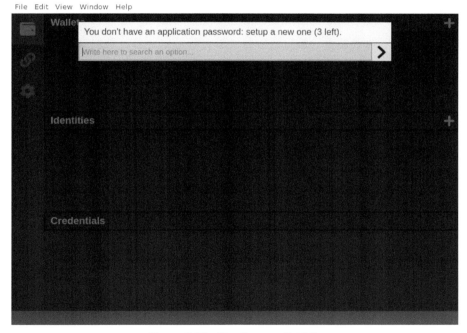

Figure 5.12 Creating a wallet 1/3.

Create a wallet named i3Market, type HD SW Wallet, and i3Market network – see Figure 5.13.

Figure 5.13 WEB-RI interface.

5.7 Creating a Wallet 2/3

Create a consumer and/or provider identity (right-click over the i3Market wallet) — Figure 5.14:

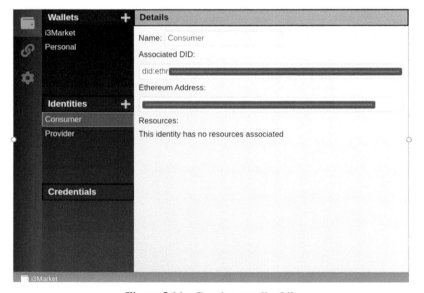

Figure 5.14 Creating a wallet 3/3.

5.8 Register a New OIDC Client

Access to your local instance of WEB-RI (i3-MARKET GUI) available in http://localhost:5300/ and you will be able to see what is shown in Figure 5.15:

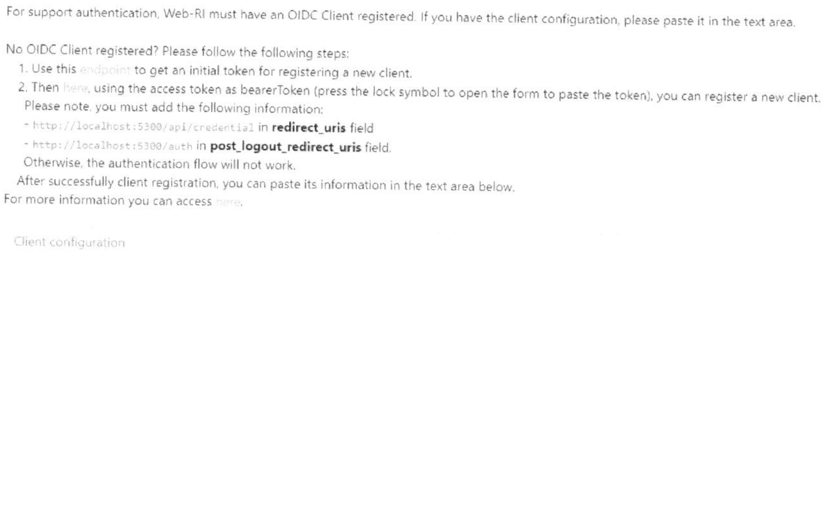

For support authentication, Web-RI must have an OIDC Client registered. If you have the client configuration, please paste it in the text area.
No OIDC Client registered? Please follow the following steps:
1. Use this endpoint to get an initial token for registering a new client.
2. Then here, using the access token as bearerToken (press the lock symbol to open the form to paste the token), you can register a new client.
Please note, you must add the following information:
- http://localhost:5300/api/credential in redirect_uris field
- http://localhost:5300/auth in post_logout_redirect_uris field.
Otherwise, the authentication flow will not work.
After successfully client registration, you can paste its information in the text area below.
For more information you can access here.
Client configuration

Figure 5.15 OIDC client configuration.

Note: The OIDC client configuration is automatically done from the WEB-RI. Figure 5.16 enables the interaction directly through the SDK-RI or SDK-core must do it by following the next steps.

No OIDC client registered? Please follow the following steps:

Available authorizations
BasicAuth (http, Basic)
Password
Close

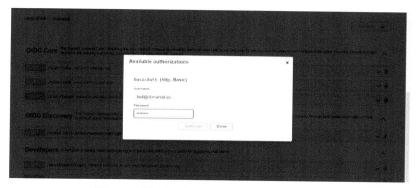

Figure 5.16 Registering an OIDC Client 1/4.

Ask your i3-MARKET admin for your corresponding "i3-MARKET OpenID Connect Provider API"[1] (by default, each instance of i3-MARKET

[1]And endpoint similar to: https://XXXX.i3-market.eu/release2/api-spec/ui/#/Developers/get_release2_developers_login

has its own provider) endpoint to get an initial token for registering a new client (authorize green button).

Try logging in and get *initialAccessToken* as shown in Figure 5.17.

Figure 5.17   Registering an OIDC client 2/4.

Use *initialAccessToken* as *bearerAuth* as shown in Figure 5.18.

Figure 5.18   Registering an OIDC client 3/4.

Then here, using the access token as bearerToken (press the lock symbol to open the form to paste the token) – see Figure 5.19 – and you can register a new client. Please note that you must add the following information:

- http://localhost:5300/api/credential in redirect_uris field
- http://localhost:5300/auth in post_logout_redirect_uris field

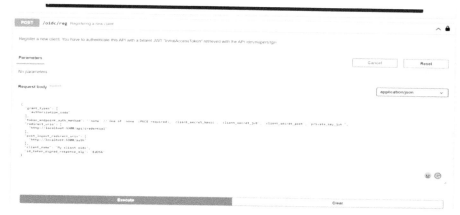

Figure 5.19   Registering an OIDC client 4/4.

After successful client registration, you can paste the returned information in the text area in Figure 5.20.

OIDC Client Configuration

For support authentication, Web-RI must have an OIDC Client registered. If you have the client configuration, please paste it in the text area.

No OIDC Client registered? Please follow the following steps:
1. Use this endpoint to get an initial token for registering a new client
2. Then here, using the access token as bearerToken (press the lock symbol to open the form to paste the token), you can register a new client.
   Please note, you must add the following information:
   - http://localhost:5100/api/credential in **redirect_uris** field
   - http://localhost:5100/auth in **post_logout_redirect_uris** field
   Otherwise, the authentication flow will not work.
   After successfully client registration, you can paste its information in the text area below.
For more information you can access here.

```
{
  "application_type": "web",
  "grant_types": [
    "authorization_code"
  ],
  "id_token_signed_response_alg": "EdDSA",
  "post_logout_redirect_uris": [],
  "require_auth_time": false,
  "response_types": [
    "code"
  ],
  "subject_type": "public",
  "token_endpoint_auth_method": "client_secret_jwt",
  "introspection_endpoint_auth_method": "client_secret_jwt",
  "revocation_endpoint_auth_method": "client_secret_jwt",
  "require_signed_request_object": false,
  "request_uris": [],
  "client_id_issued_at": 1652285147,
```

Figure 5.20   OIDC client registered.

Generate credentials for the consumer/provider identity:

Start the authentication workflow from local WEB-RI instance by following the steps illustrated in Figures 5.21– 5.28
    Provide a username for consumer role:

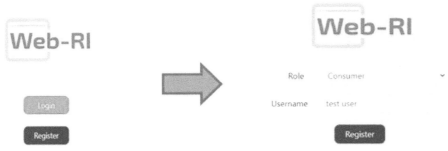

Figure 5.21   Username screen.

Wallet pairing:

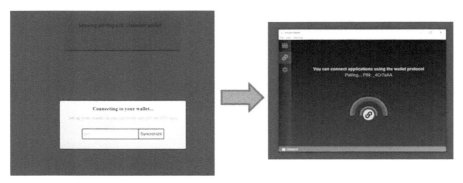

Figure 5.22   Pairing wallet.

Select wallet identity:

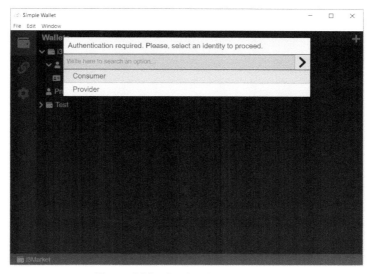

Figure 5.23 Configuring wallet 1/2.

Add Verifiable Credentials to the wallet:

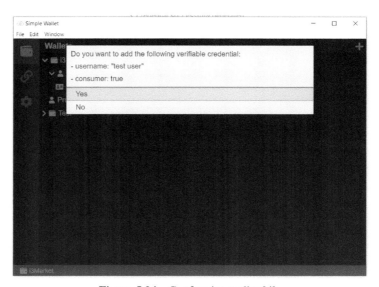

Figure 5.24 Configuring wallet 2/2.

Login using credentials generated previously:

Role Consumer

Figure 5.25 Login in WEB-RI.

Selective disclosure:

Figure 5.26 Selective disclosure.

Sign:

Figure 5.27 Signing with the wallet.

Access finally to the GUI of Web-RI:

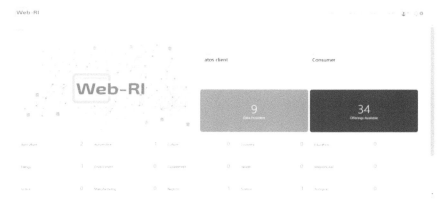

Figure 5.28 Accessing WEB-RI.

5.9 SDKs

Technical requirements:

The current subsection contains a set of SDK requirements that have been collected for releases 2 and 3. Most of them have been extracted from D2.5 [3]; meanwhile, the other ones are the result of deepening in the last iterations of SDK elicitation process.

SDK-core:

The SDK-core is built using SDK-generator REST API and an Ansible playbook in charge of generating all the client stubs for Backplane API (semantic engine, notification manager, and smart contract manager), OIDC, VC, and Data Access API encapsulated into the SDK-core Java/JavaScript library.

SDK-core specification:

Backplane API SDK: The main goal of the SDK is boasting the Backplane API to create applications for the i3-MARKET platform. It will assist the data marketplaces and stakeholder developers with a set of tools, examples, and documentation, which will reduce the developing effort to be part of the i3-MARKET ecosystem. The Backplane API SDK content is divided into different logical modules, which correspond to each of the i3-MARKET modules integrated in the Backplane API. In the following, the different modules identified for the first version of the requirement specification can be seen:

- ○ User-centric authentication SDK
- ○ Cloud Wallet SDK module
- ○ Data access SDK module
- ○ Standard payments SDK module
- ○ Tokenization SDK module

   Enhanced Backplane API SDK: For some cases, the SDK will complete the Backplane API services with its own logic to support the developers in the use of the i3-MARKET capabilities. These will be done through a set of workflows.

   Automatically build Backplane API SDK: In addition to the inner SDK functionality, i3-MARKET will provide mechanisms to automatically build the SDK component and it will be offered in different programming languages.

SDK-core implementations:

The SDK-core implementation is based on the usage of SDK-generator, and it is described in detail in the following subsections.

Core technology:

The SDK-core is supported by means of (a) the SDK-generator REST API and (b) an Ansible playbook in charge of generating:

- An SDK-core Java artifact that contains client stub for Backplane API (semantic engine, notification manager, and smart contract manager), OIDC (OpenID Connect), VC (Verifiable Credentials), and data access API.
- An SDK-core JavaScript artifact contains client stub for Backplane API (semantic engine, notification manager, and smart contract manager), OIDC, VC, and data access API.

SDK-generator:

The SDK-generator is the main pillar of the SDK-core. The SDK-generator is based on SDK as a service approach. SDK-generator aims to automatically generate the client stubs needed to interact and consume all the functionalities exposed in a REST API. The SDK as a service approach is shown in Figure 5.29.

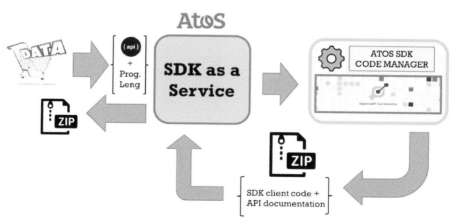

Figure 5.29   SDK-generator approach.

The workflow behind SDK-generator is based on the provision of a programming language specification next to an OAS file and making use of the OpenAPI generator server, which is able to produce as output SDK client stubs next to associated documentation about how to use it.

The languages supported by the SDK-generator are shown in Figure 5.30 as part of the SDK as a service configuration.

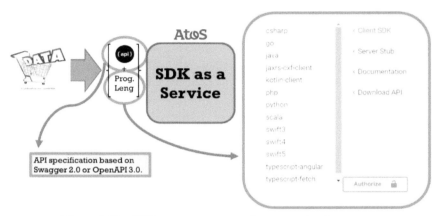

Figure 5.30   SDK generator supported programming languages.

Continuous integration and delivery:

The SDK-core artifact is automatically provided by means of a CI/CD pipeline based on Ansible AWX. A conceptual view of SDK-core pipeline is shown in Figure 5.31.

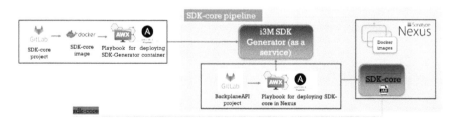

Figure 5.31   SDK-core CI/CD pipeline.

As initial step in the pipeline, the SDK-core artifact is triggering the compilation and deployment of a new version of the SDK-generator once a commitment into master branch of SDK-generator project happens. As a second step (represented as green area in Figure 5.31 - SDK-core CI/CD pipeline), the generation and publishing of a new version of the SDK-core artifact is triggered by using a new version of backplane API which is deployed each time the SDK-core artifact is triggered. The CI/CD behind backplane API includes a triggering to the SDK-core pipeline. In this way, SDK-core covers a set of tasks mainly in charge of generating SDK-core artifacts for Java and JavaScript versions taking a set of relevant OAS files associated with the following artifacts:

- Backplane API (including semantic engine, notification manager, and smart contract manager)
- OIDC API
- Verifiable Credentials API
- Data access API

Finally, the pipeline includes a couple of tasks in charge of publishing the generated Java and JavaScript versions of SDK-core into i3-MARKET Nexus repository.

SDK-core installation:

SDK-core is a Java/JavaScript library that is installed by simply importing from i3-MARKET official Nexus repository.

SDK reference implementation (SDK-RI):

The current section reports on SDK-reference implementation specification, its implementation, and, finally, its deployment and installation.

6

SDKs and WEB-RI

6.1 Approach

The SDK global approach for i3-MARKET is based on the provision of four main pillars: (a) SDK-generator, (b) SDK-core, (c) SDK reference implementation or SDK-RI, and, finally, (d) Web-RI.

The layered SDK approach defined here is the mechanism that allows to adapt and extend existing data marketplaces to interface with the i3-MARKET Backplane.

Specifically, the layers that are part of the proposed solution for the SDK and shown in Figure 6.1 are the following:

- **SDK-core:** This layer aims to simplify the i3-MARKET SDK building process by generating client stubs for any i3-MARKET backend endpoint/API, defined with the OpenAPI (formerly known as Swagger) specification. In this way, therefore, the development team can better focus on the implementation and adoption of these backend endpoints or APIs.
- **SDK-reference implementation (SDK-RI):** This layer aims to identify and provide a set of common services to be implemented for consuming available Backplane functionalities.
- **SDK-execution patterns (SDK-EP):** It is including the atomic functions that make use of Backplane API (via SDK) adding some business logic.
- **Web-RI:** It is supporting the front-end or GUI integrating the common services provided by the SDK-RI and that can be reused and customized as part of the pilot specification and implementation defined in the context of WP5.

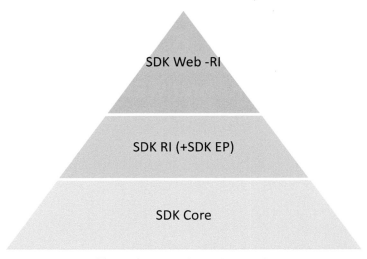

Figure 6.1   SDK layered approach.

6.2 SDK-Core Specification

General objectives:

The three main objectives identified are the following:

(a) Backplane API SDK
(b) Enhanced Backplane API SDK
(c) Automatically build Backplane API SDK

Considering the objectives, the following updates in terms of capabilities have been provided for the i3-MARKET FINAL release.

(a) Backplane API SDK. Addressing fully following modules:

- User-centric authentication SDK
- Cloud Wallet SDK module
- Data access SDK module
- Standard payments SDK module
- Tokenization SDK module
- Smart contracts SDK module
- Notifications SDK module
- Rating SDK module

(b) Enhanced Backplane API SDK
(c) Automatically build Backplane API SDK

Context:

The updated context in terms of interactions with other SW pieces in the i3-MARKET ecosystem is shown in Figure 6.2.

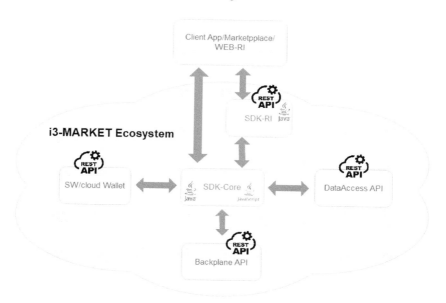

Figure 6.2 SDK-core interactions.

As a reminder, the i3-MARKET SDK-core interacts with:

i. Backplane API, allowing stakeholder's developers to create software (App Client) based on the (Backplane) API, in an easy and efficient way.
ii. Cloud Wallet to guarantee the security on the interactions between the stakeholders and i3-MARKET Backplane.
iii. App Client, allowing to be part of the i3-MARKET ecosystem.

Big picture:

The SDK-core is supported as a main pillar for the SDK-generator, which is one of the outcomes of i3-MARKET solutions.

The main updates on SDK-generator are the following:

(a) Update on the *openapi-generato*r client due to issues detected managing keywords *oneOf, anyOf*, and *allOf* in some of the OAS files supported by i3-MARKET backend services.

(b) Update on the *openapi-generator* setup. The concrete setup used in last version was: *openapi-generator-cli generate -g javascript –additional-properties=groupId={{ ARTIFACT_GROUP_ID }},artifactId={{ ARTI-FACT_NAME }},artifactVersion={{ ARTIFACT_VERSION }}, modelPackage=com.i3m.model.data-access,apiPackage=com.i3m.api. data-acess, prependFormOrBodyParameters=true, hideGenerationTimestamp=true -o /tmp/oas/javascript -i http://xx.xx.x.xxx:yyyy/repository/i3m-raw/i3m-raw/files/dataaccessapi.json –generate-alias-as-model –skip-validate-spec"*

This is the same setup for SDK-core Java version but using "*java*" for the option "- g".

6.2.1 SDK-core implementation

As introduced, the SDK-core is built using SDK-generator REST API and an Ansible playbook in charge of generating all the client stub for Backplane API (semantic engine, notification manager, and smart contract manager), OIDC, VC, and data access API encapsulated into the SDK-core Java/JavaScript library.

6.2.2 Core technology

The SDK-core implementation is based on the usage of SDK-generator, and it is described in detail in the following subsections.

The SDK-core is supported by means of (a) the SDK-generator REST API and (b) an Ansible playbook in charge of generating:

1) an SDK-core Java artifact that contains client stub for Backplane API (semantic engine, notification manager, and smart contract manager), OIDC (OpenID Connect), VC (Verifiable Credentials), and data access API;

2) an SDK-core JavaScript artifact that contains client stub for Backplane API (semantic engine, notification manager, and smart contract manager), OIDC, VC, and data access API.

SDK-generator:

The SDK-generator is the main pillar of the SDK-core. The SDK-generator is based on SDK as a service approach. SDK-generator aims to automatically generate the client stubs needed to interact and consume all the functionalities exposed in a REST API. The SDK as a service approach is shown in Figure 6.3.

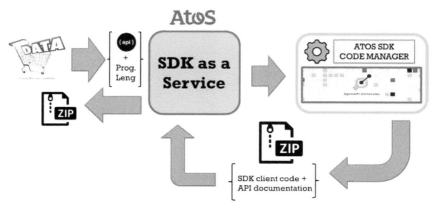

Figure 6.3   SDK-generator approach.

The workflow behind SDK-generator is based on the provision of a programming language specification next to an OAS file and making use of the OpenAPI generator[1] server, which is able to produce as output SDK client stubs next to associated documentation about how to use it.

The languages supported by the SDK-generator are shown in Figure 6.4.

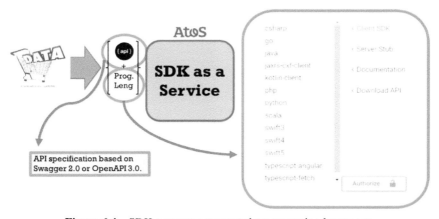

Figure 6.4   SDK-generator supported programming languages.

---

[1] OpenAPI generator: https://github.com/OpenAPITools/openapi-generator

Continuous integration and delivery:

The SDK-core artifact is automatically provided by means of a CI/CD pipeline based on Ansible AWX. A conceptual view of SDK-core pipeline is shown in Figure 6.5.

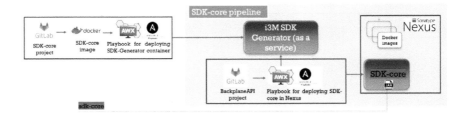

Figure 6.5   SDK-core CI/CD pipeline.

As initial step in the pipeline, the SDK-core artifact is triggering the compilation and deployment of a new version of the SDK-generator once a commit into master branch of SDK-generator project happens. As a second step (represented as a green area in Figure 6.6), the generation and publishing of a new version of the SDK-core artifact is triggering each time a new version of the Backplane API is deployed. The CI/CD behind Backplane API includes a triggering to SDK-core pipeline. In this way, SDK-core covers a set of tasks mainly in charge of generating SDK-core artifacts for Java and JavaScript

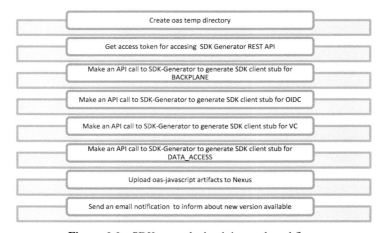

Figure 6.6   SDK-core playbook internal workflow.

versions taking a set of relevant OAS files associated with the following artifacts:

- Backplane API (including semantic engine, notification manager, and smart contract manager)
- OIDC API
- Verifiable Credentials API
- Data access API

Concretely, the Ansible playbook is used to automatize the process of generation of the SDK-core client stub.

The internal workflow covered by the SDK-core playbook is shown in Figure 6.6.

Finally, the pipeline includes a couple of tasks in charge of publishing the generated Java and JavaScript versions of SDK-core into i3-MARKET Nexus repository.

SDK-core installation:

SDK-core is a Java/JavaScript library that is installed by simply importing from i3-MARKET Nexus repository.

6.3 SDK Reference Implementation (SDK-RI)

The SDK-RI implementation is based on Java and Swagger framework, and the following subsections are focusing on the SDK-RI specifications. SDK-RI is a web app deployed within Jetty and encapsulated in a Docker container.

The SDK-RI has been updated in terms of common services as per the following (see Figure 6.7):

i) Notification manager common services: The functionalities related with notification services and queues are listed in Figure 6.7.

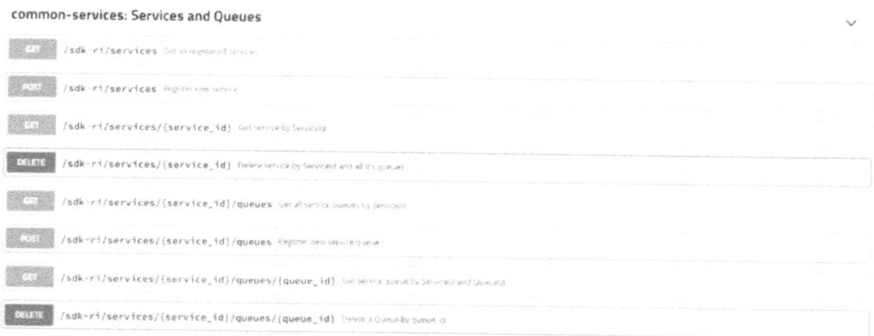

Figure 6.7   Services and queues common services.

ii) Alerts common services: The functionalities related with alerts are listed in Figure 6.8.

Figure 6.8   Alerts common services.

iii) Conflict resolution common services: This is listed in Figure 6.9.

Figure 6.9   Conflict resolution common services.

iv) Contracts common services: The functionalities related with smart contracts management are listed in Figure 6.10.

Figure 6.10   Contracts common services.

v) Credential common services: The functionalities related with authentication, identities, and credentials are listed in Figure 6.11.

Figure 6.11 Credentials common services.

vi) Exchange common services: The functionalities related with data exchange are listed in Figure 6.12.

Figure 6.12 Exchange common services.

vii) Notification common services: The functionalities related with notifications are listed in Figure 6.13.

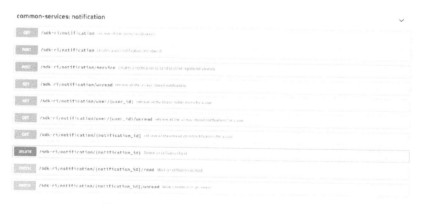

Figure 6.13 Notification common services.

viii) Offering management common services: The functionalities related with data offering management are listed in Figure 6.14.

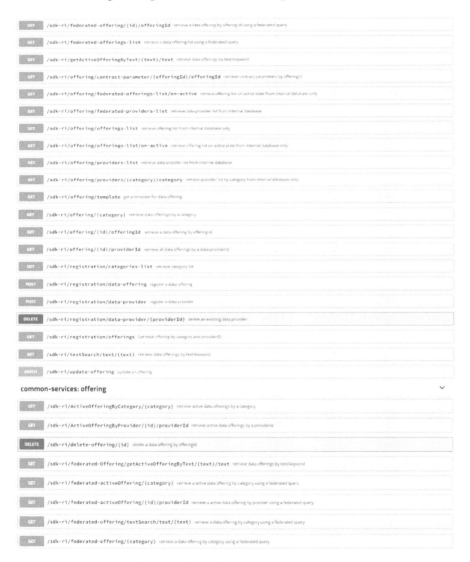

Figure 6.14   Offering common services.

ix) Pricing managing common services: The functionalities related with pricing managing are listed in Figure 6.15.

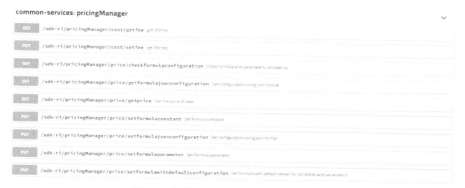

Figure 6.15 Pricing common services.

x) Token managing common services: The functionalities related with token management are listed in Figure 6.16.

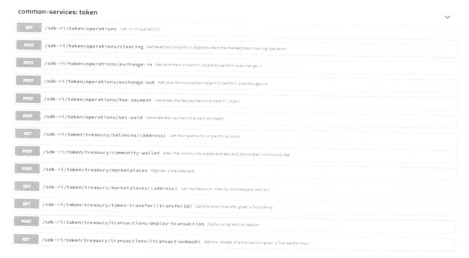

Figure 6.16 Token common services.

As an initial stage, the SDK-RI imports the last version of the SDK-core published in i3-MARKET Nexus maven repository as a library. It is precisely in this part where the way to generate the Java version of the imported SDK-core library has been slightly updated. As a second stage, once a commit is done into master branch of SDK-RI Git project, a compilation and deployment of a new version is automatically launched.

6.4 WEB-RI

The Web-RI is a GUI web interface that allows the users to interact with the functionalities provided by i3-MARKET Backplane solutions on top of the SDK-RI. It can be reused and customized as part of each pilot specification and deployment integration as a reference implementation of the backbone data marketplace to facilitate stakeholder needs that want to reuse i3-MARKET artifacts and functionalities.

6.4.1 Purpose

The WEB-RI proposes itself as a reference for the implementation of a user interface to allow human users to use and interact with the functionalities provided by i3-MARKET. The WEB-RI has three main objectives, which are:

- As a management tool, to allow i3-MARKET developers to test their functionalities in the context of a user usage.
- As a marketing team, allowing the promotion and demonstration of i3-MARKET functionalities using a generic approach and language that can be easily translated to the available data marketplaces used by different domains.
- As a reference implementation, providing functional examples of how the i3-MARKET SDKs can be used to implement/integrate i3-MARKET functionalities into a data marketplace. As a reference implementation, WEB-RI is also a useful tool to help i3-MARKET pilots on the implementation of their use-case scenarios and on testing of Backplane technologies by providing specifications and code that can be used.

In Figure 6.17, the architecture of WEB-RI is represented.

A consumer or a provider can access WEB-RI[2] via internet browser and proceed with the authentication for which the wallet[3] must be installed and running on his personal computer. The authentication process is executed on WEB-RI frontend by calling the OIDC service, which will call the wallet to perform the authentication itself.

The WEB-RI frontend is connected to a backend, which has two main functions: manage user sessions and have a way to interact with the functionalities provided by i3-MARKET.

---

[2] https://gitlab.com/i3-MARKET-V3-public-repository/i3-MARKET-web-ri
[3] https://gitlab.com/i3-MARKET-V3-public-repository/sp3-scgbssw-i3mwalletmonorepo

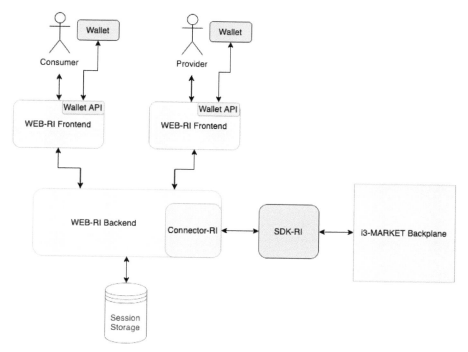

Figure 6.17 WEB-RI architecture.

To manage the user sessions, the WEB-RI backend saves the user session in a session storage called connect-mongo[4].

To interact with the functionalities provided by i3-MARKET, a library was implemented, called Connector-RI[5]. This connector has all the methods needed to call the respective APIs from the SDK-RI, which have the functionalities to interact with the i3-MARKET Backplane. This allows to have a clean and simple WEB-RI backend where it is only needed to call the respective methods from the connector.

Sitemap:

In Figure 6.18, the sitemap of WEB-RI is represented.

WEB-RI is composed of several pages, which are Authentication, Homepage, Offerings, Search, and Notifications.

---

[4] https://github.com/jdesboeufs/connect-mongo
[5] https://gitlab.com/i3-MARKET-V3-public-repository/i3-MARKET-connector-ri

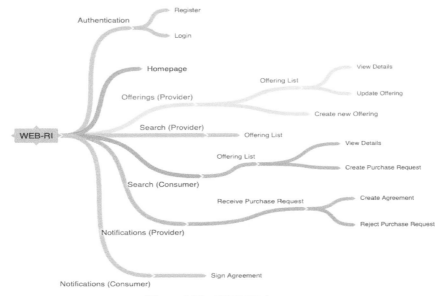

Figure 6.18   WEB-RI sitemap.

In the Authentication page, the user has the possibility to register a new provider or consumer and log in with some existing user registered in WEB-RI.

The Homepage is the main page of WEB-RI, which has a navigation bar that allows the user to navigate to the other available pages. Also, there are statistics related with the number of offerings and providers.

The Offerings page is only visible to a provider, where he can manage the offerings registered by him and register new ones.

The Search page is visible either to a provider or a consumer. The only difference is that a consumer has the possibility to create a purchase request for the offering he searched.

In the Notifications page, a provider can receive a purchase request for some of its offerings and he can accept (and create the agreement) or reject it. A consumer can sign the agreement if it was accepted before by the provider.

6.5 IMPLEMENTATION

In the following subsections, some screenshots of each page are presented, and an explanation of its content is given.

Register:

Figure 6.19 shows the WEB-RI register page.

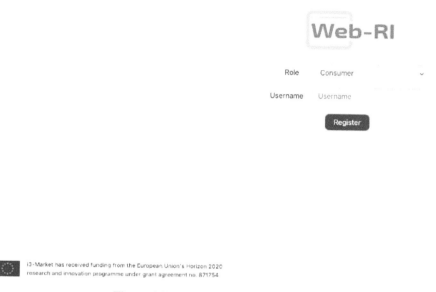

Figure 6.19 WEB-RI registration page.

Before the WEB-RI page is opened for the first time, the user must have the wallet running on his personal computer. When the user opens the WEB-RI initial page, he will see the page for registering a new user. He must select the desired role (consumer or provider) and username – Figure 6.20.

After that, the user must confirm the addition of the new user in the wallet; see Figure 6.20.

Login:

Figure 6.21 shows the WEB-RI login page.

With a user is registered in the wallet, it is possible to authenticate in WEB-RI. The user must select the role (consumer or provider) he wants to use to login in the system. After having selected the role in the login page, the user must confirm the authentication in the wallet; see Figure 6.22.

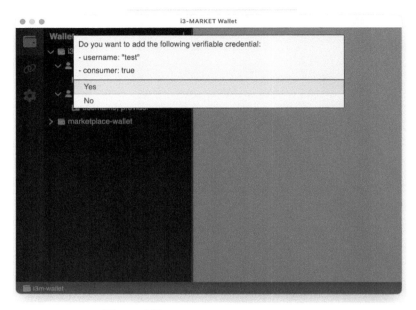

Figure 6.20   WEB-RI register with wallet.

Figure 6.21   WEB-RI login page.

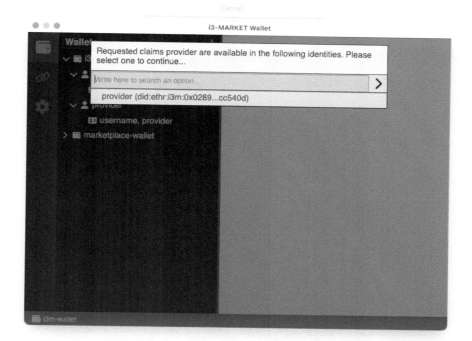

Figure 6.22   WEB-RI login with wallet.

6.6 Navigation:

With successful login, the user accesses the WEB-RI homepage. This page has a navigation bar, which is different to each role. The provider has access to offerings, search, and notifications pages and account options; instead, the consumer has access to same pages but not to the offerings page.

In Figure 6.23, the navigation bar for a provider is presented.

Figure 6.23   WEB-RI navigation (provider).

Figure 6.24 presents the navigation bar for a consumer.

Figure 6.24   WEB-RI navigation (consumer).

Homepage:

In Figure 6.25, the WEB-RI home page is presented.

Figure 6.25   WEB-RI home page.

Besides the navigation bar, the WEB-RI home page has also the information about the logo and details about the user logged-in (username and role).

As main information, WEB-RI also shows the total number of providers and active offerings available in the whole marketplace ecosystem. Also, it is possible to see the total number of active offerings filtered by each category.

Offerings:

As mentioned before, the provider has access to the offerings page. The next subsections will describe each page related to the offerings.

Offering list:

Figure 6.26 shows the page with the list of offerings of a provider.

Figure 6.26 WEB-RI offerings page.

In this page, the provider sees the list of the offerings that were registered by him. Each offering is displayed in a react-bootstrap card[6] with some information like title, description, number of contracts, and state (active, inactive, to be deleted, or deleted).

Also, the provider has the option to register a new offering, which will be described in the following sections.

Offering details:

Figure 6.27 represents the page with the details of an offering.

---

[6] https://react-bootstrap.github.io/components/cards/

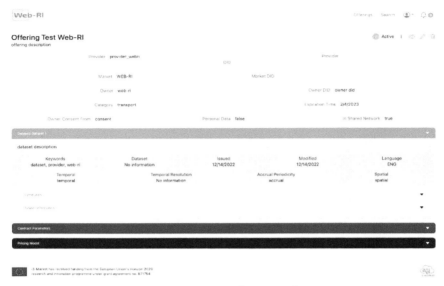

Figure 6.27   WEB-RI offering details page.

When a specific offering card is selected, it will open a new page with the details of the offering. Here, a user can see all the information related with that offering.

Since there is too much information to be displayed in a single page, a react-bootstrap accordion[7] was used to display information like dataset, contract parameters, and pricing model. This information is collapsed by default but can be expanded as well.

This page can be seen by a provider (through offerings page) or consumer (with search). If the user is a provider, he has options to activate, update, or delete the offering (in the top right corner of the site, next to the offering state). Instead, if he is a consumer, he has a button called "Buy Offering", which allows to initiate the process of creating a data purchase request.

Offering registration:

Figure 6.28 represents the page to register a new offering or update an existing one.

---

[7] https://react-bootstrap.github.io/components/accordion/

Figure 6.28 WEB-RI offering registration page.

The provider can register a new offering or update an existing one (but only the offerings registered by him). This page shown in Figure 6.29 is used for both purposes; the only difference is, when updating an offering, all the fields are already filled.

Since there is a lot of information associated with an offering, a react-bootstrap tab[8] was used on this page. With the help of the tabs, all fields were grouped by categories, which are general, dataset, pricing model, and contract parameters.

Also, inside each tab, some accordions were used to better display all the input fields to the user.

Offering purchase request:

Figure 6.29 represents the page where a consumer can initiate the process of buying a new offering.

---

[8] https://react-bootstrap.github.io/components/tabs/

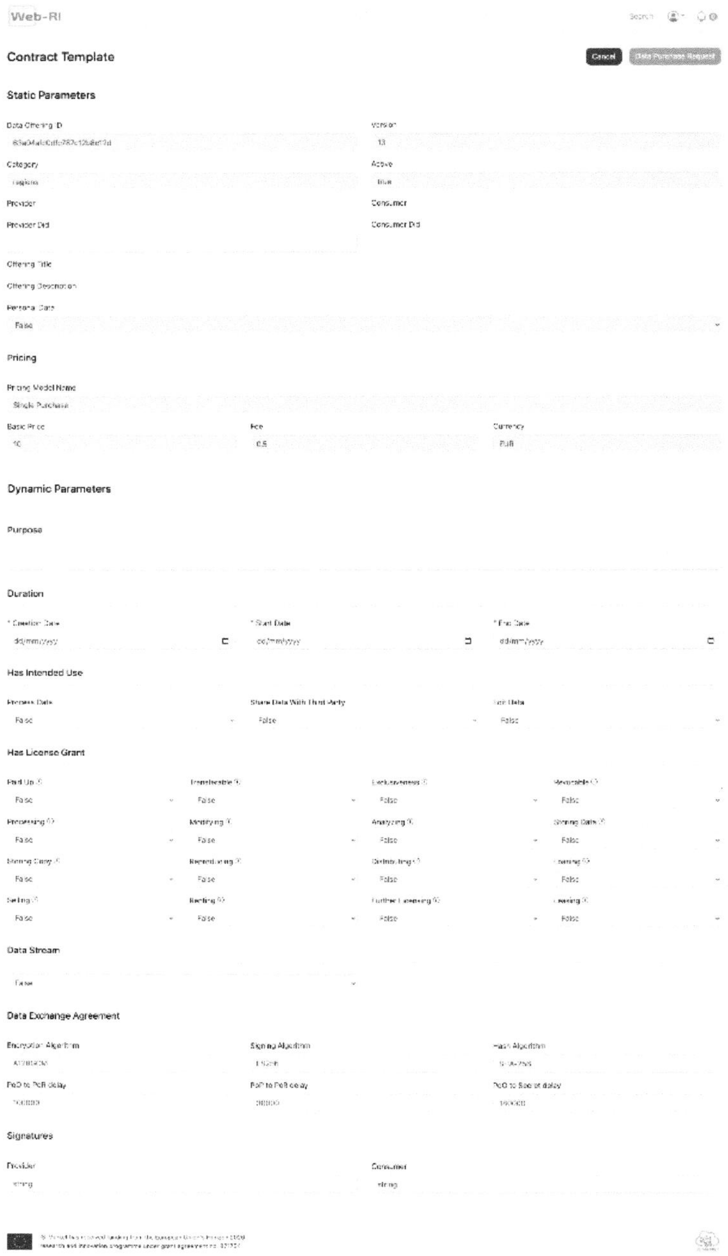

Figure 6.29   WEB-RI offering purchase page.

After the consumer selects the "Buy Offering" button in offering details page, a new page will be displayed with the contract template for that offering. In this page, the consumer must fill in the dynamic parameters of the template and then click on the "Data Purchase Request" button to proceed with the process of buying an offering.

Search:

Figure 6.30 represents the page where a user (provider or consumer) can search for offerings.

Figure 6.30   WEB-RI search page.

In the search page, the user (consumer or provider) can search for active offerings available in the whole marketplace ecosystem. He can search offerings by category, provider, or free text. As mentioned in the image above, the search is executed by entering a free text and returns the offerings that match the search criteria.

Notifications:

Figure 6.31 represents the page where a user can see his notifications.

Figure 6.31   WEB-RI notifications page.

This page has all notifications associated with the user who is logged-in in WEB-RI.

If the provider is logged-in, he can receive notifications about a purchase request regarding some of his offerings. In this case, if he accepts the proposal, a new page will be displayed where the provider can create a new agreement. But he also can reject the proposal by sending some comments justifying the rejection of the proposal (this will be sent as a notification to the respective consumer).

If the consumer is logged-in, he can receive notifications about data purchase requests that were rejected by the provider or about proposals that were accepted and then he must sign the agreement.

Account:

This option, represented by a person icon in navigation bar, shows some options in a dropdown. One of those options allows the user to log off from WEB-RI.

7

Deployment Tools

The deployment specification should define execution architecture of systems that represent the assignment (deployment) of software artifacts (i3-MARKET building blocks) to deployment targets (usually nodes).

Nodes represent either hardware devices or software execution environments. They could be connected through communication paths to create network systems of arbitrary complexity. Artifacts represent concrete elements in the physical architecture.

Once the deployment has been provided, a complementary specification would be necessary to define how to deploy software within the i3-MARKET ecosystem. In the context of i3-MARKET, we will be referring to this specification as management operative specification.

This chapter gives guidance on how the solutions for deploying i3-MARKET software are defined within the i3-MARKET instances as part of the deployment operative. The i3-MARKET operative considers four possible deployment scenarios categorized as manual or automated deployments and oriented towards i3-MARKET developers and/or data spaces and/or data marketplaces infrastructure administrators.

For the deployment and management operative, Ansible and Zabbix have been proposed as configuration, management, and monitoring tools, respectively, for the central environment. It is left to the stakeholders to decide which tools will be used and deployed for managing and monitoring the marketplace instances.

7.1 Solution Design

A four-layer stack has been defined for i3-MARKET: at the lowest layer, there is the Cloud provisioning and management layer (Figure 82). On top of that, a DevOps software layer is placed for assembling all the software used for the CI/CD process. Then, a third-party software layer is in charge of giving support to the i3M-core artifacts, which can be found at the top level of the stack.

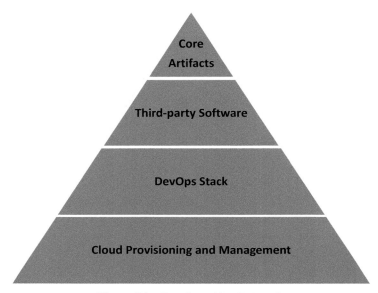

Figure 7.1 Four-layer i3M SW stack.

Depending on the environment to be deployed, it might be deployed on one layer or another. More details on the specific software deployed on each environment are given in the following sub-sections.

The target audience are the i3-MARKET project developers who are participating in the development and deployment of the i3-MARKET Backplane.

The i3-MARKET operative considers four possible deployment scenarios, categorized into manual and automatized deployments. These scenarios are the following:

- Manual deployment scenario one (MDS1)
- Automatized deployment scenario with Ansible (ADS1)
- Automatized deployment scenario with Ansible and GitHub CI/CD (ADS2)
- Automatized deployment scenario with Docker Compose (ADS3)

Considering an i3-MARKET user role perspective, the main roles involved in the different deployment scenarios are:

- i3M root instance admin

- i3M SW developer
- i3M third-party SW admin
- i3M pilot instance admin

Table 7.1 provides the mapping between the i3-MARKET user roles and the previously listed deployment scenarios:

Deployment scenario/user role	I3m root instance admin	i3M SW developer	i3M third-party SW admin	i3M pilot instance admin
MDS1	✗	✓	✓	✓
ADS1	✓	✗	✓	✓
ADS2	✗	✓	✗	✓
ADS3	✓	✓	✗	✓

Table 7.1   Deployment scenarios and i3M user roles mapping.

The following subsections describe in detail each identified deployment scenario.

7.1.1 MDS1: manual deployment

The manual deployment scenario one (MDS1) is based on accessing the physical resources by establishing an SSH connection. Once the physical resource is accessed, the user proceeds with the SW deployment manually. An overview of MDS1 is provided in the following picture. The actors involved in these scenarios are i3M SW developer and i3M third-party SW admin (Figure 7.2).

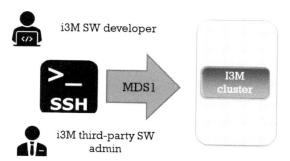

Figure 7.2   MDS1.

7.1.2 ADS1: automated deployment with Ansible

Automated deployment scenario one (ADS1) is based on the provision of a set of Ansible playbooks containing deployment recipes. Playbooks are one of the core features of Ansible and tell Ansible what to execute. They are like a to-do list for Ansible that contains a list of tasks. Playbooks contain the steps which the user wants to execute on a concrete physical resource, and they are run sequentially.

From an operative point of view, actors involved in this scenario must cover the following deployment workflow:

1) Create an Ansible template (playbook) with concrete deployment instructions using the physical resources specified.
2) Start an Ansible job by instantiating the playbook template provided in step 1.

An overview of ADS1 is provided in the following picture. The actors involved in this scenario are i3M IT admin and i3M third-party SW admin (Figure 7.3).

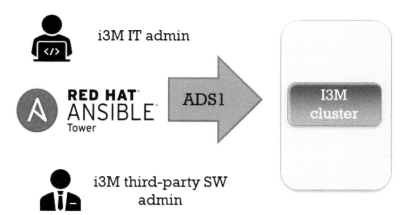

Figure 7.3 ADS1.

Finally, Figure 7.4 contains a playbook example showing the main structure in terms of tags to be included i3-MARKET playbooks, which are: name, hosts, vars, and tasks.

```
---
name: install and configure DB
hosts: testServer
become: yes

vars:
    oracle_db_port_value : 1521

tasks:
-name: Install the Oracle DB
    yum: <code to install the DB>

-name: Ensure the installed service is enabled and running
service:
    name: <your service name>
```

Figure 7.4   Ansible playbook example.

7.1.3 ADS2: automated deployment with Ansible and CI/CD GitHub pipelines

Automated deployment scenario two (ADS2) is based on the provision of CI/CD pipelines with Ansible and GitHub.

An overview of ADS2 is provided in Figure 7.5. The only actor involved in this scenario is i3M SW developer (Figure 7.5).

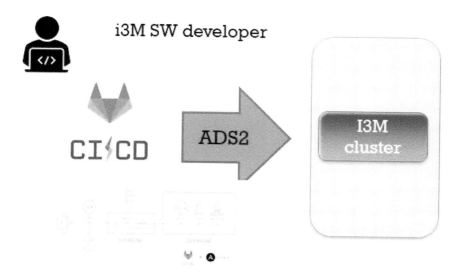

Figure 7.5   ADS2.

The goal to reach in the current deployment scenario should be aligned with i3-MARKET DevOps strategy and based on the provision of an Ansible Tower CI/CD architecture.

Considering the approach presented at the CI/CD Ansible Tower and GitHub sites [78], Figure 7.6 illustrates what we should build to support CI/CD in i3-MARKET using Ansible and GitHub.

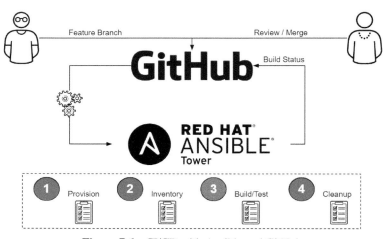

Figure 7.6　CI/CD with Ansible and GitHub.

As is well known, the main purpose of CI is of course to protect the master branch so that it always compiles. The only way to do this is to check the code in another branch (like a function branch), test that code, review the code, and only merge it with the master once all tests pass. The architecture above achieves exactly that and does so with a very simplified approach that leverages Ansible Tower as our CI engine. For the CD part, only a few additional workflows would be needed to implement artifacts generated by the CI process in dev -> test -> production. Using this architecture, one could use the GitHub versions to store artifacts. GitHub has the ability to trigger a webhook when the latest version is updated, which in turn could trigger an Ansible Tower CD workflow.

7.1.4 ADS3: automated deployment with Docker Compose

The last way of automatizing the deployments on i3-MARKET is by means of Docker Compose[1]. After the last release of the deployment strategy adopted

---

[1] https://docs.docker.com/compose/

by i3-MARKET of having *N* decentralized i3-MARKET instances + 1 master i3-MARKET instance for centralizing some services, a deployment for supporting the installation of an i3-MARKET instance (a decentralized node) has been created based on Docker Compose. This Docker Compose is used for deploying and managing multiple Docker containers, each of them containing different core and decentralized services developed by i3-MARKET.

This mechanism allows any marketplace to deploy an i3-MARKET "pilot environment" in order to be part and interact with the i3-MARKET ecosystem. Therefore, ADS3 becomes the most useful deployment strategy for supporting i3-MARKET pilots in the deployment of those i3-MARKET services, which need to be decentralized and installed in the pilot premises. These services are: "Backplane" (Backplane API component), "tokenizer" + "pricing-manager" (Monetization component), "sdk-ref-impl" (SDK-RI component), "web-ri" + "mongo_web-ri" (Web-RI), "oidc-provider-app" + "oidc-provider-db" (Service-centric authentication component), "vc-service" (User-centric authentication component), semantic-engine + semantic-engine-db (Semantic engine component), data_access (Data access component), auditable-accounting (Auditable accounting component), besu (Blockchain network pilot node), cockroachdb-node (Distributed storage component), conflict-resolver-service (Conflict resolution component), rating (Rating Component), and "keycloak" (Security server component).

In terms of the Docker Compose file definition, a set of "env.*component*" files has been created for storing config information relative to the deployment of each of the services contained in the Docker Compose file.

Besides installing the decentralized services by means of the Docker Compose file, the administrator of the pilot infrastructure must install a wallet.

Interaction with i3-MARKET can be done in several ways:

– By using the API of the Backplane, the SDK-RI or using the SDK-core libraries to integrate our application.
– By using the Web-RI.
– By managing an instance (pilot-side or central) of i3-MARKET. More details on this usage can be seen in the marketplace instance administration.

Marketplaces must be accepted to join the federation. Currently, the rules of the federation have been decided and are defined as part of the following section for the summary onboarding process. Once a marketplace is part of i3-MARKET, it can issue credentials to its consumers, providers, and data owners.

7.2 i3-MARKET: Onboarding Process

This process describes the onboarding steps for installing an operative node (pilot environment) that allows a pilot being able to interact with other marketplaces inside the i3-MARKET ecosystem. It is a practical guide that makes use of the automated deployment based on Docker Compose (ADS3) commented in the previous section.

The required steps are:

1) Clone i3-MARKET deployment repository
2) Login into i3-MARKET Nexus and Git repos
3) Execute Docker Compose
4) Install i3M Wallet
   Go to Wallet[2] and download the version suitable for your operating system and do the following actions for:
   - Windows operating system:
     - Download and execute wallet desktop.
     - The application is a standalone RAR file. Extract it and execute the i3M Wallet.exe file.
   - MacOS operating system:
     - Open the dmg file and install the wallet desktop application.
   - Linux operating system:
     - For Debian-based systems, you can use the deb package:
       - # change x.x.x for the version.
       - sudo dpkg-i wallet-desktop-x.x.x-amd64.deb.
5) Create a wallet and a consumer and/or provider identity in the wallet.
   The first time a user initiates the application, a dialog asking for a password appears. The user will have to introduce this password each time the application starts.
   Create a wallet named i3-MARKET, type HD SW Wallet, and i3-MARKET network.

---

[2]https://github.com/i3-MARKET-V3-Public-Repository/SP3-SCGBSSW-I3mWalletMonorepo/releases

Create a Consumer and/or Provider identity (right-click over the i3-MARKET wallet).

6) Register a new OIDC client.

Access your local instance of WEB-RI (i3-MARKET GUI) available in http://localhost:5300/.

Note: The OIDC client configuration is automatically done from the WEB-RI. Just those who are interacting directly through the SDK-RI or SDK-core must do it by following the next steps:

No OIDC client registered? Please follow the below steps:

   i. Ask your i3-MARKET admin for your corresponding "i3-MARKET OpenID Connect Provider API"[3] (by default, each instance of i3-MARKET has its own provider) endpoint to get an initial token for registering a new client (authorize green button)

      ○ Try logging in and get *initialAccessToken*.
      ○ Use *initialAccessToken* as *bearerAuth*.

   ii. Then here, using the access token as bearerToken (press the lock symbol to open the form to paste the token), you can register a new client. Please note that you must add the following information:

      ○ http://localhost:5300/api/credential in redirect_uris field
      ○ http://localhost:5300/auth in post_logout_redirect_uris field

After successful client registration, you can paste the returned information in the text area.

7) Generate credentials for the consumer/provider identity.

Start the authentication workflow from local WEB-RI instance by following next steps:

   a. Provide a username for consumer role
   b. Wallet pairing
   c. Select wallet identity
   d. Add Verifiable Credentials to the wallet
   e. Login using credentials generated previously
   f. Selective disclosure
   g. Sign
   h. Access finally to GUI of Web-RI.

---

[3] And endpoint similar to: https://XXXX.i3-MARKET.eu/release2/api-spec/ui/#/Developers/get_release2_developers_login

8

SDK-RI Specification

8.1 Objectives

The SDK reference implementation, or SDK-RI, has these specific objectives:

- Provide the mechanisms in terms of SW pieces for testing the i3-MARKET Backplane services/artifacts.
- Follow the approach SDK-RI as a service: SDK-RI will be a set of services needed for simulating an i3-MARKET-ized data marketplace behaviour.
- SDK-RI will let the pilots check this reference implementation as a guide/example for developing their own integration with i3-MARKET.
- Context: SDK-RI contextualization was already introduced in section 6.2 as part of the SDK-core.

8.2 Technical Requirements

The current subsection contains a set of SDK requirements that have been collected for releases 2 and 3; meanwhile, the other ones are the result of deepening in the last iterations of SDK elicitation process.

8.3 SDK Reference Implementation

The SDK-RI implementation is based on Java and Swagger framework, and the next subsections are focusing on the update provided during R2 and R3 developments. The SDK-RI was first released as a web app deployed within Jetty and encapsulated in a Docker container then later in R2 and R3 updated with Java and Swagger.

8.4 Core Technology

In an initial stage of SDK-RI implementation, the technology options presented in Figure 8.1 − Implementation technologies for SDK-RI − were considered:

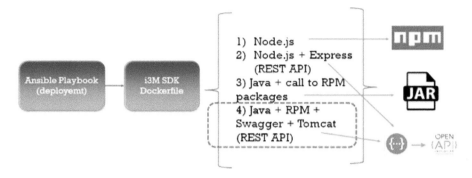

Figure 8.1   SDK-RI Implementation Technologies Used.

To sum up, the candidate technologies to support the implementation of SDK-RI were the following:

- Node.js
- Node.js + Express
- Java + RPM
- Java + Swagger + Tomcat

Finally, option 4 was selected but substituting Jetty for Tomcat as web application server. Therefore, we can conclude by saying that SDK-RI is a web app deployed within Jetty and encapsulated in a Docker container.

8.5 Continuous Integration and Deployment

The SDK-RI artifact is automatically provided by means of a CI/CD pipeline based on Ansible AWX. A conceptual view of SDK-core pipeline is shown in Figure 8.2 – SDK-RI pipeline.

As initial stage, the SDK-RI is imported as a library in the last version of the SDK-core published in i3-MARKET Nexus maven repository. As a second stage, once a commit is done into the master branch of SDK-RI GitLab project, a compilation and deployment of a new version of SDK-RI is carried out.

Figure 8.2 SDK-RI pipeline based on Ansible AWX.

SDK-RI installation:

The setup instructions and Docker-based deployment of SDK-RI is covered in detail in the following subsections.

Setup:

Clone the repository and download the dependencies:
git@gitlab.com:i3-market/code/sdk/i3m-sdk-reference-implementation.git

Running the SDK-RI with Docker:

Use Docker to run the SDK-RI. To do so, follow the same setup instructions as above.

Then, just build your SDK-RI project nd run it using the jetty images as follow:

SDK-RI container is built over a Jetty image and the SdkRefIMpl war file is deployed into Jetty.

Finally, just go to http:/$deploy_host/SdkRefImpl for accessing SDK-RI REST API.

Configuring and using SDK-RI

To configure SDK-RI instance, the following steps should be covered:

- The marketplace will have all the common services exposed in an SDK-RI/endpoint.

Each marketplace end-user, which pursues making use of the SDK-RI, should configure the SDK-RI by means of:

- pointing to the Backplane endpoint(s) hosted in a concrete i3-MARKET node (i.e., Backplane API node1, OpenID Connect Provider API node1, Verifying and Credential service API node1);
- pointing to the wallet endpoint hosted locally.

This configuration should be defined in the SDK-RI properties file placed at ''src/resources/sdk_ri_config.properties''.

The internal workflow covered by the SDK-core/RI playbook is shown in Figure 8.3.

Annex B (SDK-core/RI playbook) contains the last version of Ansible playbook that supports the generation of the SDK-core/RI for the *final* release (or R3).

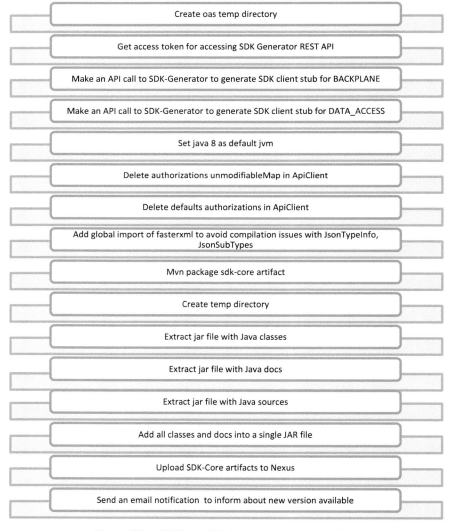

Figure 8.3 SDK-core/RI playbook internal workflow.

9

SDK-RI Installation using Docker

The SDK-RI is fully dockerized and the container is built over a Jetty image and deploys the *SdkRefIMpl* war file into Jetty.

The SDK-RI image is built automatically as part of the CI/CD pipeline and pushed to the i3-MARKET Docker image supported by means of Nexus.

To build manually the SDK-RI Docker image, the following steps should be followed:

i) Image build:

```
docker     build     --build-arg     --no-cache     -t     registry.gitlab.com/i3-
market/code/sdk/i3m-sdk-reference-implementation/sdk-ri:version . --build-arg
BACKPLANE_URL=http://backplane:3000 --build-arg OIDC_URL=https://identity1.i3-
market.eu/xxx   --build-arg   VC_URL=https://identity1.i3-market.eu/xxxx/vc/api-
spec/ui --build-arg DATA_ACCESS_URL=http://xx.xxx.x.xxx:3100
```

ii) Image push:

```
docker       push       registry.gitlab.com/i3-market/code/sdk/i3m-sdk-reference-
implementation/i3market-sdk-ri:version
```

iii) Run container:

```
docker   run   --name   sdk-ri   -p   8181:8080   registry.gitlab.com/i3-
market/code/sdk/i3m-sdk-reference-implementation/i3market-sdk-ri:version
```

As a reminder and in line with the tagging approach reported in D4.8 [5], "*version*" is formatted as *MAJOR.MINOR.PATCH* and each part changes according to the following rules.

We increment:

- *Major* when breaking backward compatibility.
- *Minor* when adding a new feature that does not break compatibility.
- *Patch* when fixing a bug without breaking compatibility.

As part of the setup in step i) to configure SDK-RI instance, the following endpoints should be provided to link them to the SDK-RI instance: Backplane URL, OIDC URL, Verifiable Credentials (VC) URL, and finally data access URL.

9.1 Setup

Clone the repository and download the dependencies:

```
git@gitlab.com:i3-market/code/sdk/i3m-sdk-reference-implementation.git
```

9.2 Running the SDK-RI with Docker

You can use Docker to run the SDK-RI.To do so, follow the same setup instructions as above.

Then, just build and run using:

```
docker build --no-cache -t i3m/i3market-sdk-ri:latest .
docker push i3m/i3market-sdk-ri:latest
docker run --name sdk-ri -p 8181:8080 i3m/i3market-sdk-ri
```

SDK-RI container is built over a jetty image and deploys the SdkREfIMpl war file into jetty.

Finally just go to http:/$deploy_host/SdkRefImpl for accessing SDK-RI REST API.

9.3 Configuring and using SDK-RI

- The marketplace will have all the common services exposed in a SDK-RI/endpoint.
- Each marketplace end-user, who pursues making use of the SDK-RI, should configure the SDK-RI by means of:
  - ○ pointing to the Backplane endpoint(s) hosted in a concrete i3-MARKET node (i.e., Backplane API node1, OpenID Connect Provider API node1, and Verifying Credential service API node1);
  - ○ pointing to the wallet endpoint hosted locally.

- This configuration should be defined in the SDK-RI properties file placed at "src/resources/sdk_ri_config.properties".
- An example of setup could be the following:
  - backplane.url = xxxx
  - oidc.url = xxxx
  - verifiable_credentials.url = xxxxx

10

WEB-RI

10.1 Purpose

The WEB-RI proposes itself as reference for the implementation of a user interface to allow human users to use and interact with the functionalities provided by i3-MARKET. The WEB-RI has three main objectives, which are:

- As a management tool, to allow i3-MARKET developers to test their functionalities in the context of a user usage.
- As a reference implementation, providing functional examples of how the i3-MARKET SDKs can be used to implement/integrate i3-MARKET functionalities into a data marketplace. As a reference implementation, WEB-RI is also a useful tool to help i3-MARKET pilots on the implementation of their use-case scenarios and on testing of backplane technologies by providing specifications and code that can be used.

10.2 Architecture

In Figure 10.1, the architecture of WEB-RI is represented.

A consumer or a provider can access WEB-RI[1] via internet browser and proceed with the authentication for which the wallet[2] must be installed and running on his personal computer. The authentication process is executed on WEB-RI frontend by calling the OIDC service which will call the wallet to perform the authentication itself.

---

[1]https://gitlab.com/i3-market-v2-public-repository/i3-market-web-ri
[2]https://gitlab.com/i3-market-v2-public-repository/sp3-scgbssw-i3mwalletmonorepo

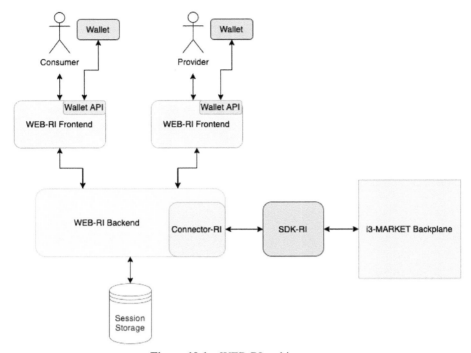

Figure 10.1   WEB-RI architecture.

The WEB-RI frontend is connected to a backend, which has two main functions: manage user sessions and have a way to interact with the functionalities provided by i3-MARKET.

To manage the user sessions, the WEB-RI backend saves the user session in a session storage called connect-mongo[3].

To interact with the functionalities provided by i3-MARKET, a library was implemented, called Connector-RI[4]. This connector has all the methods needed to call the respective APIs from the SDK-RI, which have the functionalities to interact with the i3-MARKET Backplane. This allows to have a clean and simple WEB-RI backend where it is only needed to call the respective methods from the connector.

---

[3] https://github.com/jdesboeufs/connect-mongo
[4] https://gitlab.com/i3-market-v2-public-repository/i3-market-connector-ri

10.3 Sitemap

In Figure 10.2, the sitemap of WEB-RI is represented.

WEB-RI is composed of several pages, which are Authentication, Homepage, Offerings, Search, and Notifications.

In the Authentication page, the user has the possibility to register a new provider or consumer and login with some existing user registered in WEB-RI.

The Homepage is the main page of WEB-RI, which has a navigation bar that allows the user to navigate to the other available pages. Also, there are statistics related with the number of offerings and providers.

The Offerings page is only visible to a provider, where he can manage the offerings registered by him and register new ones.

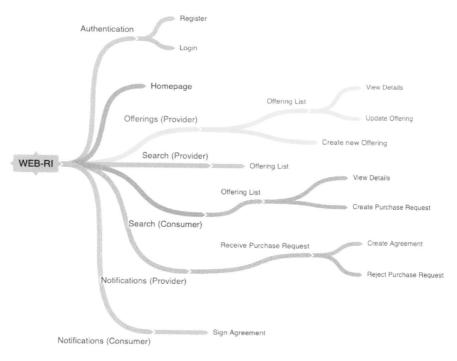

Figure 10.2 WEB-RI sitemap.

The Search page is visible either to a provider or a consumer. The only difference is that a consumer has the possibility to create a purchase request for the offering he searched.

In the Notifications page, a provider can receive a purchase request for some of its offerings and he can accept (and create the agreement) or reject it. A consumer can sign the agreement if it was accepted before by the provider.

10.4 Run WEB-RI in Docker

The WEB-RI can be reused and customized, in order to do so run the WEB-RI docker, to get the code, use git clone command, the web-ri code available at (https://github.com/i3-Market-V3-Public-Repository/WRR-WebRI), first you must define the following environment variables in docker-compose.yml file:

```
environment:
SDK_RI_ENDPOINT: sdk-ri endpoint
MONGO_URL: mongodb url
OIDC_URL: oidc provider
VC_URL: verifiable credential service
MARKET_NAME: market of notification service

MONGO_INITDB_ROOT_USERNAME:
mongodb username
MONGO_INITDB_ROOT_PASSWORD:
mongodb password
```

Then,

```
docker-compose up
```

11

Central Administration Guide

This chapter aims to describe in detail how to configure and maintain an i3-MARKET central instance.

11.1 Cloud Management

In this section, an approach is presented for successfully deploying, configuring, and monitoring centralized core services of i3-MARKET. This approach is based on the usage of Ansible Tower[1] as a key pillar for managing the cloud resources. With Ansible Tower, we can control the i3-MARKET central infrastructure (see Figure 11.1) with a visual dashboard, role-based access

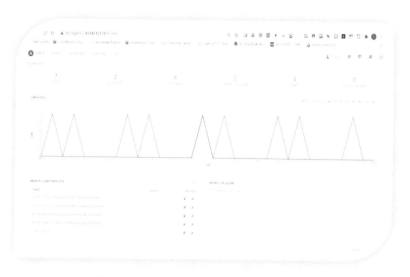

Figure 11.1 Ansible Tower dashboard view.

---

[1] Ansible tower: https://www.ansible.com/products/tower

control, job scheduling, integrated notifications, and graphical inventory management. The Ansible Tower dashboard is shown in Figure 11.1.

Regarding the last version of i3-MARKET, the proposed approach is based on the definition of a physical resource inventory in Ansible, in order to be able to automate the deployments of central artifacts. In line with the i3-MARKET Docker Deployment, the i3-MARKET physical inventory is composed of physical resources, whose nomenclature is based on allocated physical resources as it is shown in the Figure 11.2 and explained

- I3M-PH-Node1, I3M-PH-Node2, and I3M-PH-Node3: These three nodes contain three different instances of i3-MARKET that act as development environments and testing purposes for the i3-MARKET developers.
- I3M-PH-Node4: Physical node 4 contains master Besu node, Cockroach data base which hosts the "Seed Index" for federating queries, Rocks data base central instance of the blockchain, security services for allowing authentication and authorization capabilities to the central node and notification manager.

Finally, the publication of a new resource inventory is shown in Figure 11.2.

Figure 11.2   Ansible resource inventory definition view.

11.2 Infrastructure Monitoring

As part of the i3-MARKET deployment management plan, a monitoring approach based on the integration of Prometheus and Grafana with Ansible as the official configuration management tool for the i3-MARKET infrastructure was proposed.

The idea behind this was to take advantage of the Ansible Tower and the metrics provided via the API and feed them into Grafana by using Node Exporter and Prometheus.

Following the approach explained in [5], Ansible Tower must be configured to provide metrics for Prometheus to be viewed via Grafana. In addition to that, Node Exporter is used to export the operating system metrics to an operating system (OS) dashboard in Grafana. The data flow is outlined in Figure 11.3.

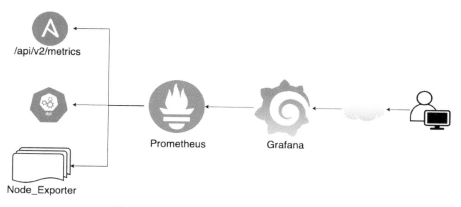

/api/v2/metrics

Node_Exporter

Prometheus   Grafana

Figure 11.3 Ansible Tower metrics data flow.

As it is reflected in the diagram, Grafana looks for data in Prometheus. Prometheus itself collects the data in its database by importing them from Node Exporters and from the Ansible Tower APIs.

Figure 11.4 shows an updated approach based on Zabbix that was proposed at M15 and adopted as official approach for i3-MARKET monitoring.

Zabbix[2] is an open-source monitoring software tool for diverse IT components, including networks, servers, virtual machines (VMs) and cloud services. Zabbix provides monitoring metrics, among others network utilization, CPU load, and disk space consumption.

Zabbix is used to monitor the following in i3-MARKET common infrastructure:

---

[2] Zabbix: https://www.zabbix.com/

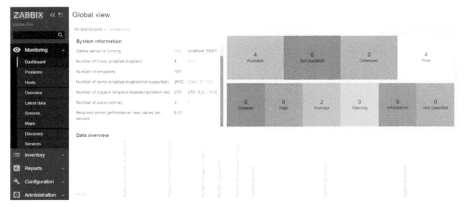

Figure 11.4   i3-MARKET Zabbix instance.

- Simple checks to verify the availability and responsiveness of backplane and other public endpoints associated with core centralized i3-MARKET services.
- A Zabbix agent was installed in each one of the i3-MARKET cluster physical nodes to monitor statistics such as CPU load, network utilization, disk space, etc.
- Docker container monitoring using the Zabbix agent type 2 deployed in i3-MARKET physical nodes.

12

Repositories and Open Source

The i3-MARKET Consortium is committed to contributing to a reference implementation (community release) of the individual building blocks as well as the overall i3-MARKET data market frameworks corresponding to their market APIs to the developer community through an open-source project.

The i3-MARKET Consortium will address the open-source community along with the dissemination events, and two hackathons are organized during the project period. The hackathons will be aligned with the releases of the i3-MARKET marketplace. Hackathons, on the one hand, allow engaging new stakeholders in i3-MARKET and, on the other hand, allow retrieving quick and contextual feedback about its usability, business potential, and attractiveness. The success of the hackathons will be key since we strongly believe that first-hour enthusiastic users are the ones that best disseminate and spread the project's results through social networks.

The open-source management project structure has been updated to reach the developers and entrepreneurs (SMEs) communities largely and facilitate their onboarding or innovation processes. i3-MARKET followed an open-source path using two of the most well-known and established open-source organizations, which provide open-source projects hosting: GitLab and GitHub. We have studied the options to have better impact and acceptance in the developers and SME's communities and adopted the procedure and roles for the users of our i3-MARKET open-source project in a way that suited best to the i3-MARKET case.

i3-MARKET project governance process defines a support and evaluation process to include software improvements as follows:

- **Request for changes or updates**: A technical board identifies any change requests prior to a *major* release, which should be integrated into this *major* release. Before a release, all changes have to be tested by using a pre-production/staging approach.

- **The evaluation of any type of technical request**: A technical board approves a software component or initiates a project in i3-MARKET OSS.
- **The communication of the results from technical experts:** A tagging release strategy as described in Section 5.3 is used in order to indicate the impact of the changes made on the i3-MARKET ecosystem.
- **Evaluation of contributions for new commits:** A technical board assesses and evaluates the contributions including documentation in i3-MARKET OSS.
- **Reports and changes report:** A technical board issues a short report, explaining the rationale of the acceptance or the rejection in exceptional cases.

The i3-MARKET team aims to facilitate and simplify development of data services based on i3-MARKET Backplane, and any developer should be capable of implementing and developing data services based on i3-MARKET backplane tools. The i3-MARKET open-source team provides the slack tool (i3-market.slack.com) for a direct communication and conversations with the developers team; the slack channel is used as a direct communication channel and it is open to any developer that is part of the i3-MARKET community but also for those external that want to start engaging with the project. The community can join the i3-MARKET slack channel and start reviewing the selected topics and also initiate new ones. i3-MARKET slack open-source has served as main channel for developers to interact directly with the i3-MARKET technical development team. The slack channel facilitates access to a wide range of information about the technologies developed. i3-MARKET OSS is the first project to provide the means for setting up, managing, and using open-source channels for the different developer communities and other stakeholders providing direct support.

Developers require technical information that goes beyond high-level descriptions in a website or that a normal software project documentation can provide. The i3-MARKET project has set up an open-source developers portal as an online tool to facilitate the members of the ecosystem to get access to the materials, documentation, technical information, developers know-how, and code. The online tool of the i3-MARKET project is deployed to actively facilitate reaching out not only to the open-source community but also SMEs and entrepreneurs in order to facilitate an easy adoption and building an ecosystem around the i3-MARKET project.

The i3-MARKET project has evolved from R1 to R3 completing a planned evolution process. The documentation and specifications are released using the open-source developer portal at http://www.opensource.i3-market.eu. Videos showing the progress and use of the developed software tools can be accessed via the i3-MARKET YouTube channel. The community of open-source developers SMEs and entrepreneurs can now easily find instructions that are available at the i3-MARKET open source portal. This is a live portal, which is a continuous update according to the latest development of the project. The main purpose of releasing this developer-centric portal is to actively enable a channel for reaching out to the open-source community and to allow SMEs and entrepreneurs to get all the latest developments and also download and use the different i3-MARKET available software updates. More specific technical documentations about the components and systems are also available in a specific "Developer Portal" at https://i3-market.gitlab.io/code/backplane/backplane-api-gateway/backplane-api-specification/index.html.

12.1 GitLab/GitHub

The i3-MARKET repository is hosted at the GitLab11 which can be found at the following link: https://gitlab.com/i3-market/code.The i3-MARKET repository is divided in branches. The branches are divided in two thematic categories. One is the documentation (i.e., site storage hosted at the "gh-pages") and the other is the i3-MARKET source code branch. Under the source code category, various branches will exist; the two main categories are:

- Main branches with an infinite lifetime:
  - Master branch
  - Develop branch
- Supporting branches:
  - Feature branches
  - Release branches
  - Hotfix branches

The i3-MARKET strategic plan to enlarge the ecosystem and reach out the largest developers communities with this i3-MARKET public version has proceeded with success, and i3-MARKET backplane V2 is accessible in <www.gitlab.com> and www.github.com. The i3-MARKET's developers team has done an extra effort to release the V2 in these two well-known platforms as they are amongst the largest and most popular open-source communities. i3-MARKET has conducted all the necessary efforts to establish an automatic synchronization mechanism transparently and the OSS governance methodology to support members of both communities; thus, what is committed and released in one platform the other community has access to it in a matter of few minutes.

12.2 GitLab Repository

The code is available open-source via the establishment of the i3-MARKET spaces on GitLab (available at: https://gitlab.com/i3-market-v3-public-repository).

12.3 GitHub Repository

The code is available open-source via the establishment of the i3-MARKET spaces on GitHub (available at: https://github.com/i3-market-V3-public-repository).

12.4 Developers' portal with MKDocs framework

This section contains the details about the online developers support tool and documentation; sections remain the same as presented in previous version but its content has been maintained and updated continuously since its first release. The community of open-source developers SMEs and entrepreneurs can now easily find instructions that are available at the i3-MARKET open-source portal here: http://open-source.i3-market.eu/ (see Figure 12.1).

This is a live portal, which is a continuous update according to the latest development of the project. The main purpose of releasing this developer-centric portal is to actively enable a channel for reaching out to the open-source community and to allow SMEs and entrepreneurs to get all the latest developments and also download and use the different i3-MARKET available software updates.

The binaries of the different software artefacts and reference implementation modules will be found at the downloading section "Get the Code" part – see Figure 12.2.

Figure 12.1   Open-source developers portal with MKDocs.

Figure 12.2   Code repository.

12.5 Open-Source Portal

(open-source.i3-market.eu)

i3-MARKET open-source project has selected a proper governance scheme, which regulates the interactions between the members of the open-source community, including key roles and responsibilities for the development and expansion of the project's software code. i3-MARKET adopts an incremental, iterative, and evolutionary software development process, notably based on agile development techniques. To identify and define these roles, the i3-MARKET Consortium made the following decisions:

- A master-governed approach is the starting scheme associated with the establishment, governance, and initial evolution of the i3-MARKET open-source project. The goal of this decision is to ensure proper integration of the various parts of the project, at least in the initial phase of the project where some critical mass has to be developed. It is the phase where the project will be looking for good reputation among the IoT open-source communities.
- i3-MARKET members from Atos partner act as master(s) for the part of the project that concerns the lower-level sensor/ICO information acquisition and filtering, notably on the basis of the enhancements to be realized on top of the i3-MARKET Backplane.

Figure 12.3 depicts the i3-MARKET project governance process, which is defined as the support and evaluation process to include software improvements as follows:

- **Request for changes or updates:** Identify any development previous to a *major* release, which should be considered private and usually is on testing and pre-production/staging.
- **The evaluation of any type of technical request:** A technical board, PM, TM, TPMs, or WPLs approves participation; in particular, software component or initiate a project in i3-MARKET OSS.

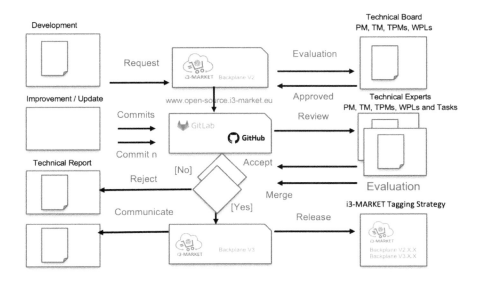

Figure 12.3 Open-source governance.

- **The communication of the results from technical experts:** A tagging version using alpha, beta, and gamma versions and then tagged as *major* is used here.
- **Evaluation of contributions for new commits:** Technical experts, PM, TM, TPMs, WPLs, and TaskLs asses and evaluate the contribution that includes documentation at the initiated project in i3-MARKET OSS.
- **Reports and changes report:** The technical board issues a short report, explaining the rational on the rejection in exceptional cases; this step can include rejects/cancel project participation.

12.5.1 Developers, users, and respective roles

Developer roles and specializations are extensively discussed in [Aalto 2013]. The relevant extracts from this discussion are presented below.

The participants of an open-source community can be divided into three groups based on their level of contributions. A joiner is someone who has just recently joined the community and does not have access to the repository yet. When that person has made his first changes to the repository, he becomes a newcomer. A developer is a fully fledged contributor that actively adds new code to the repository [von Krogh 2003].

A developer often starts out by making bug fixes that are related to his work and interests. The bug fixes are not randomly scattered around the software, but they tend to focus on the same modules. Gradually, he gains acceptance and a higher status in the community through his bug fixes and participation in discussions and debates about new features. This process characterizes how a developer becomes an expert on some part of the architecture and is able to influence its development [Ducheneaut, 2005].

Many software developers and users participate in OSS development and communities because they want to learn. The system architecture can be designed in a modularized way to create independent tasks with progressive difficulties so that newcomers can participate and move on gradually to take care of harder tasks. This approach can encourage more users to become developers. Developers at the centre of OSS communities should focus on developing the system as well as having enough attention to the creation and maintenance of a dynamic and self-reproducing OSS community [Ye 2003].

12.5.2 Roles and activities of developers and experts in the governance model

Taking as a reference the i3-MARKET project governance model described above, Figure 12.4 shows the different developers and technical experts and their impact in the i3-MARKET project governance model implementation. The developers (mainly external to the i3-MARKET team) shall follow this process playing a dynamic role in the process to further develop functionalities and/or services.

The group of experts, on the other hand, shall evaluate, approve, and issue official technical reports indicating clearly what the consequences and conditions about the decision(s) about a requested commit are. The user of the code will be notified by an announcement clearly describing the benefits or new functionalities that are ready to be used as a result of implementing the governance model process.

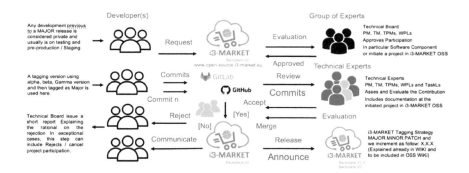

Figure 12.4 Public repository governance.

13

Other Content

The deployment process, as defined in the deployment guide section, is for the whole project process. However, if a developer wants to deploy an individual service or component, they can still do so by cloning the code from GitLab/GitHub, making changes, and then deploying either manually or using Docker Compose, for example.

Run secure data access API using docker-compose:

- Clone the repository.

```
git clone git@gitlab.com:i3-market/code/sp2/secure-data-access-api.
```

- In the project root, create a .env file to insert environment variables. You have an example in templates/template.env.
- To start secure data access API, run with this command:

```
docker-compose up –build
```

Local development components like *OpenId Provider*:
Clone the repository!

```
git clone git@ https://github.com/i3-Market-V3-Public-Repository/SP3-SSIAM-NodeOidcProvider
```

13.1 Local Development using Node.js

To run the service locally using Node.js, it is necessary to download it before. After that, you can install the dependencies and start the service in the following way:

```
$ cd node-oidc-provider/app
$ npm i
$ npm start
```

You should also update the configuration file app/src/config.ts before running the service. Specifically, it is necessary to fill the default environment variables, in the same way they are filled in the .env file.

13.2 Local Development using Docker

Run the following command in the project root. The first time, it will take a while (be patient) since it has to build images and download all the npm dependencies.

./docker-dev-start

The OAS documentation can be accessed from http://localhost:3000/oidc/api-spec/ui.

You can stop the container at any time with Ctrl-C.

If you want to delete and prune all the created images, containers, networks, and volumes, just run:

./docker-dev-prune

Since the app directory is shared with the docker container with mapped user permissions, you can just edit any files in the app directory locally. The container will be running ts-node and nodemon to directly execute the source code and refresh the server if any file has changed. You can also attach any debugger in your local machine to the container, which will be listening at default port 9229.

13.2.1 Development scripts in the docker container

Besides rebuilding, you can execute any command in the oidc-provider-app container:

- to execute it in the running container:
  docker-compose -f docker-compose.dev.yaml exec oidc-provider-app <command>.
- to create and delete on-the-fly a new container (that will update the same files):
  docker-compose -f docker-compose.dev.yaml run –rm –no-deps oidc-provider-app <command>.

14

Conclusions

The i3-MARKET Book series is a detailed compilation of all about design process, implementation work and the produced results and outcomes in the form of legacy of the i3-MARKET and Open Source Software projects.

In this third book, we concentrated in bringing the technology deployments and provide an overview of the technologies and techniques that can be used to facilitate an smooth deployment and adoption of the i3-MARKET methodologies and solutions that are the foundations of i3-MAKRET software. Additionally and to provide a complete view of the three books this section includes not only this book conclusions but serves as a compilation of all the findings and conclusions from the three books in order to list together all the advances and improvements over the state of the art that this books series is aiming to share.

The i3-MARKET project addresses the challenge of being integrative following design methods used in industry and OSS implementation best practices, interoperable by using semantic models that define a common conceptual framework and information model that enables cross-domain data exchange and sharing, intelligent from the perspective of smart contracts generated automatically and associating those financial operations into a set of software tools that facilitate that data assets can be commercialized via intra-domain or cross-domain almost transparently in a secure and protected digital market environment.

The i3-MARKET Book Series presents an overview of the i3-MARKET methodologies and solutions that are the foundations of its software results in the form of a Backplane with a set of software support tools and as a solution addressing the challenge of enabling the coexistence of data spaces with marketplaces for enlarging the European digital market ecosystem.

The i3-MARKET project provided a blueprint open-source software architecture called "i3-MARKET Backplane" that addresses the growing demand for connecting multiple data spaces and marketplaces in a secure and federated manner. The i3-MARKET Consortium is contributing with the developed software tools to build the European data market economy by innovating marketplace platforms, demonstrating with three industrial reference implementations (pilots) that a decentralized data economy and more fair growth is possible.

The first part of the i3-MARKET Book series introduces and explains the principles of the modern data economy that lead to make the society more aware about the value of the data that is produced everyday by themselves but also in a collective manner. Data Business is one of the most disruptive areas in today's global economy, particularly with the value that large corporates have embedded in their solutions and products as result of the use of data from every individual.

The i3-MARKET architecture design provides adequate and in-house developed building blocks for trustworthy (secure and reliable) data-sharing and exchange of existing data assets for current and new future market-place platforms, with special attention on commercializing data assets from individuals, SMEs, or large industrial corporations. We used and developed the i3-MARKET backplane using open-source technologies that impulse the adoption and exploit the open-source culture, a tendency that, for more than a decade, is hitting the industry markets and that today more and more industries are following.

In the second i3-MARKET series book, is discussed why data is the focus of current technological developments towards digital markets and the meaning of data being the next asset to appear evolved in trading markets. At the same time, it focused on introducing the i3-MARKET technology and the proposed solutions. In the second i3-MARKET series book, the basic technological principles and software best practices and standards for implementing and deploying data spaces and data marketplaces were introduced and explained. The second book provides a definition for data-driven society as: The process to transform data production into data economy for the people using the emerging technologies and scientific advances in data science to underpin the delivery of data economic models and services.

In this third i3-MARKET series book the best practices, software methods and mechanisms that allow the i3-MARKET backplane reference implementation to be instantiated, tested and validated are explained. This book series part concentrates in the technical experts and developers' community as a way to provide support tools and guidance in their process to integrate the i3-MARKET tools and its reference implementation. This book is offered a guidebook for technical experts and developers is addressed, the so-called industrial deployment and to provide clear understanding of the technological components and the software infrastructures. The steps to install and instantiate the i3-MARKET backplane with less efforts and to avoid overwhelm the deployment activity is also introduced. in this third part of the i3-MARKET book series, the different software technologies developed, including the use of open-source frameworks is explained. The third book can be considered the i3-MARKET handbook provisioning that i3-MAKRET backplane software can actually be used as input for configurators and developers to set up and pre-test testbeds and therefore i3-MARKEt software is also extremely valuable to organisations, scientific and academic communities to be used as a academic material.

In this i3-MARKET book series we discussed the technology assets that are designed and implemented following the i3-MARKET Backplane reference architecture (RA) that uses open data, big data, IoT, and AI design principles to help data spaces and data marketplaces to focus on todayâĂŹs datadriven society as the trend to rapidly transforming the data perception in every aspect of our activities. Moreover, the series of software assets grouped as subsystems and composed of software artefacts is included and explained in full. Further, the book series describes the i3-MARKET Backplane tools and how these can be used for supporting marketplaces and its components. The i3-MARKET Book series is an overview of the reference open-source solution to enable the data economy across different data marketplaces.

i3-MARKET

References

[1] "https://en.wikipedia.org/wiki/System_context_diagram,''[Online].

[2] P. Kruchten, "Architectural Blueprints — The "4+1" View Model of Software Architecture," IEEE Software 12, November 1995, pp. 42-50.

[3] J. R. a. I. J. G. Booch, UML User Guide, Addison-Wesley Longman, 1998.

[4] "https://leanpub.com/arc42inpractice/read,''[Online].

[5] i3-MARKET, "i3M-Wallet monorepo," [Online]. Available: https://github.com/i3-Market-V3-Public-Repository/SP3-SCGBSSW-I3mWalletMonorepo.

[6] Consensys, "MetaMask," [Online]. Available: https://metamask.io/.

[7] "Trust Wallet," [Online]. Available: https://trustwallet.com/.

[8] Exodus, "Exodus Bitcoin & Crypto Wallet," [Online]. Available: https://www.exodus.com/.

[9] T. Voegtlin, "Electrum Bitcoin Wallet," [Online]. Available: https://electrum.org/.

[10] Validated ID, "VIDChain," [Online]. Available: https://www.validatedid.com/vidchain.

[11] Evernym, "Connect.Me Wallet," [Online]. Available: https://www.connect.me/.

[12] IdRamp, "IdRamp," [Online]. Available: https://idramp.com/.

[13] trinsic, "Identity Wallets," [Online]. Available: https://trinsic.id/identity-wallets/.

[14] ConsenSys, "uPort," [Online]. Available: https://www.uport.me/.

[15] "Twala," [Online]. Available: https://www.twala.io/.

[16] ConsenSys, "Serto," [Online]. Available: https://www.serto.id/.

[17] "Veramo - A JavaScript Framework for Verifiable Data | Performant and modular APIs for Verifiable Data and SSI," [Online]. Available: https://veramo.io/.

[18] "OpenTimeStamps, a timestamping proof standard," [Online]. Available: https://opentimestamps.org/.

[19] Y. Du, H. Duan, A. Zhou, C. Wang, M. H. Au and Q. Wang, "Enabling Secure and Efficient Decentralized Storage Auditing with Blockchain," IEEE Transactions on Dependable and Secure Computing, 2021.

[20] Y. Du, H. Duan, A. Zhou, C. Wang, M. H. Au and Q. Wang, "Towards Privacy-assured and Lightweight On-chain Auditing of Decentralized Storage," 2020 IEEE 40th International Conference on Distributed, pp. 201-211, 2020.

[21] H. Yu and Z. Yang, "Decentralized and Smart Public Auditing for Cloud Storage," IEEE 9th International Conference on Software, pp. 491-494, 2018.

[22] J. Shu, X. Zou, X. Jia, W. Zhang and R. Xie, "Blockchain-Based Decentralized Public Auditing for Cloud Storage," IEEE Transactions on Cloud Computing, 2021.

[23] K. Liu, H. Desai, L. Kagal and M. Kantarcioglu, "Enforceable Data Sharing Agreements Using Smart Contracts," 27 04 2018. [Online]. Available: https://arxiv.org/abs/1804.10645.

[24] E. J. Scheid, B. B. Rodrigues, L. Z. Granville and B. Stiller, "Enabling Dynamic SLA Compensation Using Blockchain-based Smart Contracts," in IFIP/IEEE Symposium on Integrated Network and Service Management (IM), 2019.

[25] Ocean Protocol Foundation with BigchainDB GmbH and Newton Circus (DEX Pte. Ltd.), "Ocean Protocol: A Decentralized Substrate for AI Data and Services," 2019.

[26] The European Parliament and the Council of the European Union, "General Data Protection Regulation (GDPR). Directive 95/46/EC," 27 04 2016. [Online]. Available: https://gdpr-info.eu/.

[27] K. Jensen and L. M. Kristensen, Coloured Petri nets: modelling and validation of concurrent systems, Springer Science & Business Media, 2009.

[28] Digital Asset Holdings, "Digital Asset Modelling Language (DAML)," [Online]. Available: https://daml.com/.

[29] A. M. Antonopoulos, Mastering Bitcoin: unlocking digital cryptocurrencies, O'Reilly Media, Inc., 2014.

[30] I. Bashir, Mastering blockchain, Packt Publishing Ltd, 2017.

[31] D. Yaga, P. Mell, N. Roby and K. Scarfone, "Blockchain technology overview," arXiv preprint arXiv:1906.11078, 2019.

[32] S. Rouhani and R. Deters, "Security, performance, and applications of smart contracts: A systematic survey," IEEE Access, vol. 7, pp. 50759-50779, 2019.

[33] L. Jing and L. Zhentian, "A survey on security verification of blockchain smart contracts," IEEE Access, vol. 7, pp. 77894-77904, 2019.

[34] G. Wood, "Ethereum: A secure decentralised generalised transaction ledger," Ethereum Project White Paper, vol. 151, no. 2014, pp. 1-32, 2014.

[35] H. Chen, M. Pendleton, L. Njilla and S. Xu, "A survey on ethereum systems security: Vulnerabilities, attacks, and defenses," ACM Computing Surveys (CSUR), vol. 53, no. 3, pp. 1-43, 2020.

[36] "Hyperledger Besu," [Online]. Available: https://github.com/hyperledger/besu.

[37] "Solidity," [Online]. Available: https://solidity-es.readthedocs.io/.

[38] "BIP-39," 2021. [Online]. Available: https://github.com/bitcoin/bips/blob/master/bip-0039.mediawiki.

[39] i3-MARKET, "i3M-Wallet OpenApi Specification," 2022. [Online]. Available: https://github.com/i3-Market-V3-Public-Repository/SP3-SCGBSSW-I3mWalletMonorepo/blob/public/packages/wallet-desktop-openapi/openapi.json.

[40] W3C, "Decentralized Identifiers (DIDs) v1.0. Core architecture, data model, and representations," W3C Recommendation, 19 07 2022. [Online]. Available: https://www.w3.org/TR/did-core/.

[41] W3C, "Verifiable Credentials Data Model v1.1.," W3C Recommendation, 03 03 2022. [Online]. Available: https://www.w3.org/TR/vc-data-model/.

[42] F. Román García and J. Hernández Serrano, "i3M-Wallet Base Wallet," [Online]. Available: https://github.com/i3-Market-V3-Public-Repository/SP3-SCGBSSW-I3mWalletMonorepo/tree/public/packages/base-wallet.

[43] F. Román García and J. Hernández Serrano, "SW Wallet," [Online]. Available: https://github.com/i3-Market-V3-Public-Repository/SP3-SCGBSSW-I3mWalletMonorepo/tree/public/packages/sw-wallet.

[44] F. Román García and J. Hernández Serrano, "BOK Wallet," [Online]. Available: https://github.com/i3-Market-V3-Public-Repository/SP3-SCGBSSW-I3mWalletMonorepo/tree/public/packages/bok-wallet.

[45] F. Román García and J. Hernández Serrano, "Wallet Desktop," [Online]. Available: https://github.com/i3-Market-V3-Public-Repository/SP3-SCGBSSW-I3mWalletMonorepo/tree/public/packages/wallet-desktop.

[46] J. Hernández Serrano and F. Román García, "Server Walllet," [Online]. Available: https://github.com/i3-Market-V3-Public-Repository/SP3-SCGBSSW-I3mWalletMonorepo/tree/public/packages/server-wallet.

[47] J. Hernández Serrano and F. Román García, "Wallet Desktop OpenAPI," [Online]. Available: https://github.com/i3-Market-V3-Public-Repository/SP3-SCGBSSW-I3mWalletMonorepo/tree/public/packages/wallet-desktop-openapi.

[48] F. Román García and J. Hernández Serrano, "Wallet Protocol," [Online]. Available: https://github.com/i3-Market-V3-Public-Repository/SP3-SCGBSSW-I3mWalletMonorepo/tree/public/packages/wallet-protocol.

[49] F. Román García and J. Hernández Serrano, "Wallet Protocol API," [Online]. Available: https://github.com/i3-Market-V3-Public-Repository/SP3-SCGBSSW-I3mWalletMonorepo/tree/public/packages/wallet-protocol-api.

[50] F. Román García and J. Hernández Serrano, "Wallet Protocol Utils," [Online]. Available: https://github.com/i3-Market-V3-Public-Repository/SP3-SCGBSSW-I3mWalletMonorepo/tree/public/packages/wallet-protocol-utils.

[51] IDEMIA, "Video proving the integration of IDEMIA's HW Wallet into the i3-MARKET Wallet Desktop application," 2022. [Online]. Available: https://drive.google.com/file/d/1Ai_eoDIzIHczOjzOMBR4ctV5kbR05NOE/view?usp=share_link.

[52] Bluetooth SIG - Core Specification Workgroup, "Bluetooth Core Specification v2.1 + EDR: Secure Simple Pairing," 2007.

[53] D. Basin, C. Cremers, J. Dreier, S. Meier, R. Sasse and B. Schmidt, "Tamarin Prover," [Online]. Available: http://tamarin-prover.github.io/.

[54] OpenJS Foundation, "Electron," [Online]. Available: https://www.electronjs.org/.

[55] Ethers JS, "The Ethers Project," [Online]. Available: https://github.com/ethers-io/ethers.js/.

[56] Veramo, "Veramo - A JavaScript Framework for Verifiable Data," [Online]. Available: https://veramo.io/.

[57] OpenAPI, "OpenAPI Initiative," Linux Foundation, [Online]. Available: https://www.openapis.org/.

[58] "Express OpenAPI Validator," [Online]. Available: https://github.com/cdimascio/express-openapi-validator.

[59] TypeDoc, "TypeDoc," [Online]. Available: https://typedoc.org.

[60] J. Hernández Serrano, "i3-MARKET Non-Repudiation Library," 2022. [Online]. Available: https://github.com/i3-Market-V3-Public-Repositor y/SP3-SCGBSSW-CR-NonRepudiationLibrary.

[61] J. Hernández Serrano, "i3-MARKET Conflict Resolver Service," 2022. [Online]. Available: https://github.com/i3-Market-V3-Public-Repositor y/SP3-SCGBSSW-CR-ConflictResolverService.

[62] J. Hernández Serrano, "API of the i3-MARKET Non-Repudiation Library," i3-MARKET, 2022. [Online]. Available: https://github.com /i3-Market-V3-Public-Repository/SP3-SCGBSSW-CR-NonRepudiat ionLibrary/blob/public/docs/API.md.

[63] Panva, "JOSE," [Online]. Available: https://github.com/panva/jose.

[64] Ajv, "Ajv JSON schema validator," [Online]. Available: https://ajv.js.o rg/.

[65] OpenJS Foundation, "Express JS," [Online]. Available: https://expressj s.com/.

[66] Y. Kovacs, S. Stanhke and J. L. Muñoz, "i3-MARKET Smart Contracts," [Online]. Available: https://github.com/i3-Market-V3-Public-Repositor y/SP3-SCGBSSW-I3mSmartContracts.

[67] Hans van der Veer and Anthony Wiles, "Achieving Technical Interoper-ability - the ETSI Approach," in ETSI, 2008.

[68] Mike Ushold, Christopher Menzel, and Natasha Noy. Semantic Integra-tion & Interoperability Using RDF and OWL. [Online]. https://www.w3 .org/2001/sw/BestPractices/OEP/SemInt/

[69] M. Compton et al., "The SSN ontology of the W3C semantic sensor network incubator group," JWS, 2012.

[70] EUROPA. Publications Office of the EU. EU Vocabularies. Controlled Vocabularies. Authority tables. Frequency. https://publications.europa. eu/en/web/eu-vocabularies/at-dataset/-/resource/dataset/frequency

[71] EUROPA. Publications Office of the EU. EU Vocabularies. Controlled Vocabularies. Authority tables. File type. https://publications.europa.eu /en/web/eu-vocabularies/at-dataset/-/resource/dataset/file-type

[72] EUROPA. Publications Office of the EU. EU Vocabularies. Controlled Vocabularies. Authority tables. Language. https://publications.europa. eu/en/web/eu-vocabularies/at-dataset/-/resource/dataset/language/

[73] EUROPA. Publications Office of the EU. EU Vocabularies. Controlled Vocabularies. Authority tables. Corporate body. https://publications.eur opa.eu/en/web/eu-vocabularies/at-dataset/-/resource/dataset/corporate-body/

[74] EUROPA. Publications Office of the EU. EU Vocabularies. Controlled Vocabularies. Authority tables. Continent https://publications.europa.eu/en/web/eu-vocabularies/at-dataset/-/resource/dataset/continent

[75] EUROPA. Publications Office of the EU. EU Vocabularies. Controlled Vocabularies. Authority tables. Country. https://publications.europa.eu/en/web/eu-vocabularies/at-dataset/-/resource/dataset/country

[76] EUROPA. Publications Office of the EU. EU Vocabularies. Controlled Vocabularies. Authority tables. Place. https://publications.europa.eu/en/web/eu-vocabularies/at-dataset/-/resource/dataset/place

[77] European Commission. Joinup. Asset Description Metadata Schema (ADMS). https://joinup.ec.europa.eu/solution/asset-description-metadata-schema-adms

[78] CI/CD with Ansible Tower and GitHub. Available from: https://keithtenzer.com/2019/06/24/ci-cd-with-ansible-tower-and-github/

[79] Red Hat Ansible Tower Monitoring: Using Prometheus + Node Exporter + Grafana. Available from: https://www.ansible.com/blog/red-hat-ansible-tower-monitoring-using-prometheus-node-exporter-grafana

i3-MARKET

Index

A
application program interface xxxi

D
data marketplace xv, 1, 62, 79, 90, 121
data provider 39, 64
decentralized identifier xxxi, 147
distributed ledger technology xxxi

E
European commission xii, 150
European union 146

I
i3-MARKET xi, 1, 6, 8, 15, 47, 58
identity and access management xxxi, 3

J
JSON web key 23, 31
JSON web token xxxi

P
proof of origin xxxi
proof of publication xxxii

S
self-sovereign identity xxxii
service level agreement xxxii
service level specification xxxii
smart contract 74, 82, 141
smart contract manager 16, 71, 85
software development kit xxxii
state of the art 141

V
verifiable credentials 22, 71, 111

About the Editors

Dr. Martín Serrano is a recognized expert on semantic interoperability for distributed systems due to his scientific contribution(s) to using liked data and semantic formalisms like ontology web language for the Internet of Things and thus store the collected sensor's data in the Cloud. He has also contributed to define the data interplay in edge computing using the linked data paradigm; in those works he has received awards recognizing his scientific contributions and publications. Dr. Serrano has advanced the state of the art on pervasive computing using semantic data modelling and context awareness methods to extend the "autonomics" paradigm for networking systems. He has also contributed to the area of information and knowledge engineering using semantic annotation and ontologies for describing data and services relations in the computing continuum. Dr. Serrano has defined the data continuum and published several articles on data science and Internet of Things science and he is a pioneer and visionary on proposing that semantic technologies applied to policy-based management systems can be used as an approach to produce cognitive applications capable of understanding, service and application events, controlling the pervasive services life cycle. A process called bringing semantics into the box, as published in one of his academic books. He has published 5 academic books and more than 100 peer reviewed articles in IEEE, ACM and Springer conferences and journals.

Dr. Achille Zappa is a Post-Doctoral Researcher at Insight, University of Galway. He received BSC/MSC degree in Biomedical Engineering and PHD in Bioengineering from the University of Genoa (Italy), his Ph.D. project was related to semantic web integration, knowledge engineering and data management of biomedical and genomic data and his research interests include semantic web technologies, semantic data mashup, linked data, big data management, knowledge engineering, big data integration, semantic integration in life sciences and health care, workflow management, IoT semantic interoperability, IoT semantic data and systems integration. Dr. Zappa is the W3C Advisory Committee representative for Insight Centre at University of Galway and member of W3C working groups like the HCLS IG, the Web of Things (WoT) IG and WG, the Spatial Data on the Web WG. He currently work with the main Insight Linked Data and Semantic Web Groups and with the UIoT (Internet of Things, stream processing and intelligent systems unit) Research Unit, addressing collaboration with different units and involvement in various projects where he seeks to develop general-purpose linked data analytics platform(s), which enables (a) flexible and scalable data integration mechanisms and (b) flexible use and reuse of data analytics components such as visualization components and analytics methods. Dr. Zappa has an extensive expertise of applying semantic web technologies and linked data principles in health care and life sciences domains.

Mr. Waheed Ashraf is a Senior Software Engineer with extensive experience in Java programming with Spring Boot and Project Management experience with a strong background on microservices systems design and is an AWS Certified person. Mr. Ashraf is a highly skilled senior software engineer, with 10+ years of project related professional experience in developing and implementing software systems and developing and maintaining enterprise applications working for international companies from USA, Australia and Malaysia. Mr. Ashraf is also proficient in agile software development, scrum and continuous integration (Jenkins), Amazon Web Services (AWS) and back-end RDBMS (using SQL in Databases Like Oracle, DB2, MySQL 4.0 and Microsoft SQL Server). He is currently responsible for the design, development and implementation of a federated authentication and authorization infrastructure (AAI) for federated access to data providers in the context of the Federated Decentralized Trusted Data Marketplace for Embedded Finance FAME Horizon Europe project.

Dr. Pedro Maló is professor at the Electrotechnical Engineering and Computers Department (DEEC) of the NOVA School of Science and Technology (FCT NOVA), Senior Researcher at UNINOVA research institute and Entrepreneur at UNPARALLEL Innovation research-driven hi-tech SME. He obtained an M.Sc. in Computer Science and holds a Ph.D. in Computer Engineering with research interests in interoperability and integrability of (complex) systems with special emphasis on cyber-physical systems/Internet of Things. Pedro coined novel methods and tools such as the plug'n'play interoperability (PnI) solution for large-scale data interoperability and the NOVAAS (NOVA Asset Administration Shell) that establishes the guidelines and methodology for industry digitization by integrating industrial assets into a Industry 4.0 communication backbone. As an entrepreneur, Pedro initiated the development of the IoT Catalogue that aims to be the whole-earth catalogue of the Internet of Things (IoT) – the one-stop-source for innovations, products, applications, solutions, etc. to help users (developers/integrators/advisors/end-users) to take the most advantage of the IoT for the benefit of society, businesses and individuals. Pedro has 20+ years practice in the management, research and technical coordination/development of RTD and innovation projects in ICT domains especially addressing data technologies, systems' interoperability and integration solutions. Pedro is a recognized Project Manager and S&T Coordinator of European/National RTD and industry projects with skills in the coordination of both co-localized and geographical dispersed work teams operating in multidisciplinary and multicultural environments.

Márcio Mateus is project Manager at Unparallel Innovation, Lda Portugal and a Research engineer holding an M.Sc. in electrotechnical and computer engineering from the Faculty of Science and Technology of the Universidade Nova de Lisboa (FCT NOVA). Márcio is an expert in data interoperability measurement techniques and methodologies for complex heterogeneous environments.

Mr. Edgar Fries is Senior System Architect at Siemens AG, Germany. In his early career he acted as project manager and consultant at SIEMENS AG consulting in the field of engineering with a focus on engineering tools and methods for customers in the plant engineering and product business. Fries is graduated from the Technical computer science in Esslingen University of Applied Sciences.

Iván Martínez is project manager and SW architect at Atos, Spain, and a senior researcher at the ARI department of the company AtoS. He graduated in computer science from Technical University of Madrid and in the past few years he has participated in semantic web, cloud, big data and blockchain related industrial and research projects. He has contributed to national research projects such as PLATA, and other Cloud, HPC and big data related projects, such as KHRESMOI, VELaSCCo, TOREADOR, DataBench and BODYPASS mainly leading in the latter's definition and integration of system architecture.

Mr. Alessandro Amicone is an experience project manager at GFT, Italy leading both public funded and commercial market projects. In the first part of his professional career, he worked mainly in projects focusing on coordinating documents management and business process management systems for the bank and insurance industry. In recent years he has been working on Horizon2020 projects and innovative market projects promoting smart communities and technology for digital transformation for and between companies in the industry sector and research communities. The development of processes and management systems mainly focuses on advancing the state of art using software engineering for blockchain, smart contracts and distributed/self-sovereign identity, ensuring cyber-security solutions.

Justina Bieliauskaite is Innovations Director at the European Digital SME Alliance with more than 8 years of project lead and management experience (previously she worked in Lithuanian and Belgian NGOs). Justina Bieliauskaite leads the preparation and implementation of Horizon Europe, Digital Europe Programme, Erasmus+ and other tenders/service contracts for the European Commission. She is experienced in coordinating stakeholder engagement, policy analysis and recommendations, SME training, standardization, and communication activities. Justina is currently the main coordinator of the BlockStand.eu project. Currently, Justina is leading DIGITAL SME's Projects and Standardisation teams, and coordinates the internal WG DIGITALIZATION which covers AI, IoT, cloud computing, blockchain and emerging technologies, as well as coordination among digital innovation hubs. Justina holds a Master's degree in Science (cum laude), focusing on political science and international relations, from the Universities of Leiden and Vilnius. Besides her mother-tongue Lithuanian, Justina speaks English, Italian, Russian and German.

Dr. Marina Cugurra is a lawyer specializing in R&I projects, in particular in legal issues of new technologies and Information Society (e.g. AI, GDPR, data ownership, etc.), with a Ph.D. degree at the "Telematics and Information Society" Ph.D. School at University of Florence. She is also an expert in ethical and societal themes related to ICT research and technological development. She is serving as independent Ethical Expert at European Commission and European Defense Agency. Consolidated experience in national projects and international and European projects. Scientific collaboration with CNIT (National Inter-University Consortium for Telecommunications) and CNR – ITTIG (Italian National Research Council, Institute of Legal Information Theory and Techniques). Legal Advisor in the R&I Division of multinational companies. She has contributed to the activities of the legal working groups of Eu-wide initiatives (EU Blockchain Observatory Forum) and is Chair of the Ethics, Data Protection and Privacy (EDPP) Task Force of the "Citizen's Control of Personal Data" Initiative within Smart City Marketplace.